MW01264849

It's Not Serious

Ted Blankenship

Copyright © 2017 Ted Blankenship

All rights reserved.

ISBN:1979818517
ISBN-13:9781979818513

DEDICATION

This book is dedicated to my wife Dorothy and our grown children, Ann, Leslie and Tedd, son-in-law Dan and Daughter-in-law Janet. They haven't always seen my work as funny, and I can understand that. I interviewed the late Art Buchwald, humor writer, a few years ago and asked him if his family read his stuff. He said, "Sometimes, I'm not sure they know what I do for a living."

CONTENTS

The essays in this book originally appeared in The Active Age,
a newspaper for Kansans 50 and older

YOU CAN TRAIN YOUR DOG
JUST LIE DOWN AND ROLL OVER

WE WATCH THOSE SHOWS on TV where people buy and remodel houses, and we've noticed that you are not a real American family unless you have a dog or two. Most of these people won't consider a new home that the dog doesn't like.

How they know when the dog would rather keep looking is a mystery.

We have friends who have three dogs and they're looking for more. Happily, they moved to Florida. I can only hope their dogs approve of their new surroundings.

I have nothing against dogs. And, though we are dogless at the moment, we've had dogs. We did not consult them when we moved from one house to another.

I believe you should train your dog. First, you do not ask him whether the back yard is big enough or whether the fences are too high.

The dog may be your best friend, but he or she must know who is the boss. Let's assume that you are. The dog may disagree. You must convince him there is something in it for him, food and lodging for example.

First, make friends with the dog. That's easy for me because I am short and dogs can easily jump up and lick my face. If there is one thing a dog dearly loves, it is licking a face—any face. This is one of the first things you will want to teach your dog NOT to do. That's because, as you may have noticed, dogs don't give a hoot what they put in their mouths.

When your dog licks you, your first impulse will be to say, "Get Down." The dog thinks this means, "Please lick my face."

Another favorite fun thing for dogs to do is to jump on you. The muddier the paws, the more fun. You of course will shout "get down." The dog will interpret this as, "please lick my face—and jump on me again."

Animal trainers will tell you that consistency is the answer. Use the standard commands and make sure the dog obeys. The usual commands are "sit," "stay," "come," and "down."

Dogs have small vocabularies and no attention span. But, we have to start somewhere, so let's begin with "sit."

Look your dog in the eye and say "sit" like you really mean it. At first, not having mastered the new vocabulary, the dog will run around you twice, jump on you and lick your face. This is not what you want.

1

If the dog persists, lift your knee and give him a gentle rap in the chest. Try not to enjoy it. The dog will look bewildered. Going through his canine mind will be such things as, "Did I lick his face too slowly? Was my jumping lethargic? I will do better!"

This will continue into the night. Don't despair. Tomorrow you can push on the dog's rear and softly say, "sit". The dog will assume:

- You are being playful and would like to be licked in the face.
- There is a fly on his rump and you're being helpful.
- You mean it this time and he will just have to sit (unlikely).

Believe it or not, one day the dog will sit. Then you can graduate to "stay." This is a tough one because the dog will assume you are so happy that he sits on command that he will sit at all the other commands, too.

Teaching a dog to stay may try your patience. I never said it would be easy. The trouble is that to you, "stay" means "do not move an inch or you will die." To a dog it means "come here."

If the dog does what you say, pat him on the head and say, "good dog." It's called positive reinforcement.

The dog will think, "he's not telling me to stay, so I'll just lick him in the face, and if I could talk, I'd tell him he's a good boy."

THE SAFEST SAILBOAT IS THE ONE STILL AT THE DOCK

I'M A BORN KANSAN and until I was about 23, I had not seen the ocean. When I first saw a large body of salt water it was the Gulf of Mexico. So I never gave sailing much thought.

You have to have a reasonably large body of water and a sail boat to sail. Kansas farm ponds where I grew up were hardly big enough for a row boat.

Despite this lack of experience and knowledge, I bought a sail boat when our kids were young. Having read two or three books on sailing, I was pretty much an expert. I had never sailed a boat. Actually, I had never been on a sail boat.

So with the confidence of an old tar (whatever that is) I bought a 17-foot Venture. That's a boat large enough to have sleeping quarters. I don't know how anyone could sleep on one because it's difficult to doze off when you are terrified.

They say that ignorance is bliss and I was pretty blissful the first time we took the boat out. We did not take it to a large lake where there is plenty of water and the banks are far apart. We launched it at Santa Fe Lake, a body of water not much wider than the boat.

The wind was blowing at about 35 miles an hour. I should have calculated in knots, which would have been just a little over 30. It would have sounded slower.

The Venture is a sloop. It has one mast and usually two sails, a mainsail and a headsail, the smaller one in front. Sails are what get the novice in trouble. They make the boat go and boats don't have brakes.

The different ways of sailing a boat have names. I had read about them but when I had loaded the family in and the wind caught a sail I had no idea which was which and I had forgotten how to use them because I was frantically trying to stop the boat before it crashed into the opposite shore, or worse, another boat or a boat dock.

The kids were screaming, the boom was dipping into the water and my wife was huddled in a corner of the cabin.

I was turning the rudder this way and that Fortunately, I remembered a sentence in the book that said if you wanted to stop, you should let all the sails loose.

I quickly hauled the sails in and not as neatly as a good sailor should.

We paddled the boat back to the dock hoping no one would see us.

A few months later after we had learned a few things, we took the Venture to Lake Wilson. This is a lake that can produce waves high enough to strike terror in the hearts of veteran sailors. You can imagine what happens to us non veterans.

The second day we were there a storm blew in and we decided we had better get our boat out before it was too late.

I had to handle the boat (I don't know why) so my wife Dorothy had to back the trailer into the water. Dorothy is not good at backing things attached to the back of a vehicle. In fact, Dorothy is not good at backing the car up without things attached to it.

She grabbed the first startled fisherman she could find who was ready to back his trailer in and told him he could back our car and trailer in or he might be waiting for a while to get access to the ramp.

He backed our trailer in as I tried to get the boat aimed at the ramp. The wind kept blowing the boat away from our trailer, so I had some of the kids jump out and stand on the side of the ramp. We would throw them a line (that's a rope if you're not a sailor).

Our oldest daughter Ann was going with a guy who had been in the Navy so I thought he would be the best person to throw out the line.

He grabbed a line and threw it as hard as he could and it landed in the hands of one of the kids. I'm thinking, "nice job" when I realize that the other end of the line is not attached to the boat. Someone waded into the water and pushed the bow onto the trailer and the fisherman drove out with it.

On the way home I was wondering how much I could get for a 17-foot Venture. I'd throw in some life jackets, too. Or maybe I'd throw away the plug you take out to drain the bilge water. Then the next time we launched it would just sink.

AT MY AGE I CAN'T AFFORD MUCH TIME ON THE PHONE

I'M GETTING CLOSE to 90, so I consider my time pretty important. That's because there is a lot less of it than there was a few years ago.

That's why I didn't want to spend an hour of it on the phone with the cable company. Why would I want to talk to the cable company for an hour? Because my bill went up $32, and I didn't get any more service than I had when I was paying $32 less.

There was an eight-hundred number on my bill to call if I had a problem. I had a problem. I didn't want to spend $32 for nothing. I already had plenty of nothing on the channels I was getting for $200 a month which I also didn't want to pay.

In the cable company's defense, I get a bunch of channels. The trouble is most of them have nothing on them I want to watch. And, I have to watch commercials asking me to buy something I don't want.

So I called the number. The first thing I heard was words in Spanish telling me that if I wanted to speak Spanish, to press one. I didn't want to speak Spanish. So I pressed two and got a recorded voice saying that all the lines were busy and that I would be answered when everybody else quit talking. Then I was told that my call was important and to stay on the line.

Meanwhile, indescribable music was playing over and over and a recorded voice came back about every five minutes. The voice said the same things it did five minutes earlier.

The dilemma was that I wanted to hang up. But if I did, I would lose my place and have to start over. If I stayed on, it could be for five minutes or an hour or more. I stayed on.

An hour went by and finally I heard a real human voice asking me my maternal grandmother's name. I said her last name was McHone.

"That doesn't match our records," said the voice. Then she asked for my pin number.

I didn't know I had one. After several other questions that didn't work, she called me on my phone and when I answered she had an idea it was me. That was when it occurred to me that maybe she wanted my grandmother's FIRST name. It was Josie, the correct answer to the question asked a half hour earlier.

She told me she didn't have the authority to deal with my problem.

She transferred me to the Loyalty Office. I told another young woman that two years ago my bill had been about $160 per month and it suddenly jumped to $200. The same loyalty office, I said, reduced the bill to $165 a month for two years. But the bill had gradually increased to $200, and I was resigned to that amount.

Then the bill jumped to $232 and that was too much. She asked me what I watched so that she could design a program for me. I told her that I watch only a few programs.

So she added some new ones and upgraded my phone program for $200 a month. I was going over what had changed and had some other questions. She said the phone switchover would cause the phone to quit for a short time. It quit for a long time, and I couldn't get her back.

I had to go through the whole thing again, and the same music was playing and the same voice was telling me my call was important.

DON'T BARBECUE GOAT NEAR A HUNGRY DOG

IN THE FOUR YEARS I spent in San Antonio and over the years we visited relatives in South Texas, I developed a taste for cabrito. We Yankees call it young goat.

I'm certain most of you are saying, "Gugghh." I'm not sure of the spelling because it's a word I haven't seen before. But I know what you mean: "Young goat? Really?"

It's readily available in South Texas (the Rio Grande Valley) and in Mexico. It's eaten in Spain and in many African countries. It's barbecued over hot coals or baked. Either way, it's good. Its taste is somewhere between lamb and veal.

I have introduced this meat to Kansas friends and relatives with spotty results. It works best when you don't tell them what it is.

Comments usually are something like, "What is this stuff?" or "What did you do to the meat?"

The first time we served it we lived in Wichita. My neighbor Ernie and I decided it would be great fun to barbecue some cabrito.

Ernie assumed that cabrito was just a big goat. We checked around and couldn't find any ranchers who wrangled goats. Some of them wanted to know what we were going to do with a goat.

"We're going to eat it," I said.

The rancher usually put his pickup in gear and popped wheelies getting as far away as possible in the shortest amount of time.

Ernie called his brother who worked for a meat processing plant in Kansas City. He knew farmers and ranchers who could probably find two goats. He found two and had them dressed. Early on the morning of the barbecue I heard what sounded like dogs chasing a mailman.

Ernie's sons were carrying two of the biggest goats I had ever seen. They were roughly the size of a Rottweiler mixed with a Great Dane. At least three dogs were jumping up and barking and nipping at what they hoped would be lunch.

We shooed them away and I attacked the goats with a hatchet to carve out sections small enough to fit over the fire.

Just as we got the parts placed on chicken wire we had stretched over the coals, it started to rain. We put a tarp over the fire and smoked ourselves along with the goats.

The meat was a little tough and stringy and we were all red eyed but it was worth it.

We told people what it was AFTER they ate it.

Several years later I talked another neighbor into doing the goat roast. This time it was at Mike's place north of Rose Hill, a small town south of Wichita. Luckily, he had not heard of our earlier roast nor had he heard of eating goat meat.

We set up a pit of cement blocks and put chicken wire over the top. Things were going well after having started the fires at dawn. Mike and I stood over the goat and dabbed it with sauce and kept two fires going, one for the coals and the other for the goat.

It was tedious but the results would be worth it, I assured Mike.

About 4 p.m. the goat was done and we went to see if people were ready to eat and if the deviled eggs and other stuff were ready.

We went to retrieve the goat just as the family dog ran off with it. We chased him around the fish pond through the timber south of the house and down the driveway. As we ran, we looked furtively over our shoulders to see if anyone in the house was watching. The dog was not going to give up a freshly barbecued piece of meat easily.

Mike is more agile than I but hardly a match for a hungry dog.

Yet fortune smiled upon us. Mike managed to grab the tip of the dog's tail and held on. The goat was ours.

We didn't tell folks they were eating goat—and we didn't tell them the dog had sampled it first.

SHORT GUYS AREN'T THE BEST BASKETBALL PLAYERS

I HAVE NEVER been a sports writer but I feel the urge because of the run the local university made this year.

I'm a basketball lover. In particular, I'm a Kansas fan. I cheer for the Jayhawks because that's where I got my college degree. I like Wichita State, too, because I taught there for 12 years and because I lived in Wichita for more than 20 years.

I love the game for its finesse and excitement. Unfortunately, it's not as exciting as it once was because the new rules result in a lot of time at the free throw line.

I'd like to say I'm a fan because I played when I was younger. I'd like to say I made a million dollars yesterday, but that didn't happen either.

I didn't play in high school because I was not much taller than a basketball, and that made it difficult to dribble.

That doesn't mean that I didn't play a game or two. Actually, it was two. The first was in a burned out auto agency on Main Street in my home town. There was a basket bolted to what was left of a wall and the concrete floor was still intact.

Several of my friends, all of them taller than I, played in the old building two or three times a week. One day they were short a player and coaxed me into coming off the bench so to speak.

They were running this way and that, passing the ball, weaving, dribbling—and scoring. I pretty much stood very still as far from the basket as I could get. To my dismay, someone threw me the ball. I bounced it a couple of times trying for a look of arrogance, then tried to run while still bouncing it (the ball, that is). My feet got tangled and I fell on my left knee, knocking a hole in the kneecap.

I still had the ball clutched in my arms. I was ejected from the game. I wish it could have happened sooner. I remember the whole embarrassing thing well because the knee still hurts occasionally. If anyone asks, I tell them it's an old basketball injury.

My other time on the court was in 1947 when I was a freshman at Baker University.

I was a pledge at a fraternity that played intramural basketball. Once again, the team was short a player.

I don't remember which position, but since I was told to suit up, it probably wasn't center.

"But I can't play basketball," I said.

"You're a pledge," replied an active member. "Suit up."

Suiting up involved putting on a pair of shorts—any shorts—and a white tee shirt. I had a pair of basketball shoes because I played tennis (about as well as I played basketball). The shorts drooped to a point below my knees, about 50 years before that was fashionable

To my dismay, someone on my team threw the ball to me.

I froze. I did not dribble. What was I supposed to do with a basketball?

I tried to look nonchalant, like I could handle the ball but didn't want to hog it from the others. I would be unselfish and let someone else score. Unfortunately, I was so far from the rest of the team that I couldn't throw the ball to anyone except an opposing player.

I decided not to do that because it was sure to upset my teammates. Actually, they were pretty upset anyway.

I tried to double dribble but I couldn't single dribble (as far as I know).

A teammate finally got closer and I threw the ball. It rolled to a stop about six feet from him. My team grabbed a passerby and substituted him for me.

I was happy on the bench. I wondered if I could find an injury that would keep me from playing again—I would have settled for appendicitis. Or maybe I could have gone to the bathroom and climbed out a window. Luckily, the passerby could dribble and so was an automatic member of the team. I tried to figure out ways of getting him into the fraternity.

That was the end of my basketball career and I can't say I'm sorry. But a funny thing happened. I kind of liked having a basketball in my hands. So I was happy when we moved to Rose Hill south of Wichita and the house we bought had a basketball hoop on the driveway.

I bought a basketball and decided to learn to make free throws and maybe even dribble a little (for when someone was watching). The problem was that Eight-mile Creek runs through our place, down a steep hill from the basketball hoop.

If I missed the backboard, and I did— often—the ball would roll down the hill and into the creek. This wasn't so bad when the creek was dry, but when it was running the ball would float away. Someone downstream probably is wondering where all the basketballs came from. I gave up and tore down the hoop. It was sad to see it go but I no longer had to dribble.

OFFICER WILL WANT AN EXCUSE BUT YOU CAN'T GIVE HIM ONE

IT HAS BEEN 65 years since I joined the U.S. Air Force. I was accustomed to being awake at 4 a.m., but not to getting out of bed at that hour. I was yelled at when I was a late-sleeping teenager but it wasn't like being rousted by Cpl. Castleberry yelling at the top of his Alabama lungs.

I never understood what he was saying but I knew I had to do SOMETHING—fast. It was 4 a.m., and we got into our green fatigues.

We strapped on stuff that added a lot of weight, but was mostly useless. The gas mask was handy when Cpl. Castleberry herded us into a room without windows and someone filled it with tear gas.

Every morning we did calisthenics. Cpl. Castleberry yelled to someone in the dark, "Flight 5550 all present and accounted for, SIR." The "sir" always sounded like "syrup."

He never counted us because he knew we weren't going anywhere.

It didn't take us long to learn the ropes: call everyone "sir" except the guys with stripes. Salute the ones with a bar or bars on their collars. If you see a colonel, walk five miles if necessary to avoid contact. If you see a general, faint.

If you do something wrong, an officer will ask, "Why did you do such a stupid thing?"

You're thinking, hey, this isn't so bad: I didn't have time to roll my socks into little balls for inspection because I had to fold my gas mask into a little ball and hang it on the end of my bunk, and I couldn't do that because I had to make my bed so that the corporal could drop a quarter on the blanket and watch it bounce (the quarter).

That's not the way it works. Under no circumstances are you to give an officer an excuse, even though he has just asked for it. ALWAYS reply, "no excuse, sir."

Then you will be chewed out for not having an excuse. Officers love this routine. Just remember, you are never right and the officer is never wrong.

In the military, you are known by rank, last name, first name, middle initial and serial number. If you don't remember your serial number — or your name, you don't get paid. You use the name your parents gave you even if you don't recognize it.

I was Pvt. Blankenship, Elmer T., AF 17 283 421. Elmer?

Yeah, it's on my birth certificate, but no one ever called me that.

When you were ordered to show up somewhere, there was a ritual: snap to attention, smartly salute the officer behind the desk and say, "Sir, Pvt. Blankenship, Elmer T., reporting as ordered."

The captain will be perplexed. He will know who you are because you just told him. You explain why you are there, and it does not interest him at all. To get rid of you, he will order you to report to someone else.

The ritual will repeat, and you'll be lucky to make it to lunch.

When you leave the military, an officer, will plead with you to stay. He really doesn't want you to stay, it's just what he does.

By the time my four years were up I was a Staff Sergeant and Maj. Fleisch called me in.

He didn't even bring up the subject of re-enlisting. He said, "you're just not cut out for the military."

What he said made a lot of sense to me. I decided to become a civilian.

IF NOT FOR THE BRITISH HANGOVER WOULD BE MARCH 25

I'M SURE YOU'VE HEARD of ides. It's what an Englishman does when he doesn't want to be found. Well, that may be true, but it's not what I wanted to write about.

I'm referring to ides as it applies to certain months, such as "the ides of March." That's when Julius Caesar was assassinated, on March 15, 44 B.C. The Romans, of course, had no idea they were living in B.C. If you want the whole truth, we don't really know when Caesar was killed because the Romans were using the Julian calendar which Caesar himself invented.

They were using that calendar because Caesar was the boss and they had better be using it if they knew what was good for them.

All the people under Roman rule (a whole bunch then), most of Europe and most European settlements such as America used the Julian calendar until Pope Gregory XIII decided a new one was needed and it should be named after him. That was in 1582.

But back to Ides. Usually we hear of ides in such phrases as, "Beware of the ides of March." Why? Because Shakespeare needed a snappy line for the soothsayer to deliver in his play about Julius Caesar.

If you want to beware of the ides of a month, you could use several different months. Ides are the 15th day of March, May, July and October and the 13th of the others that existed in the Julian calendar.

The famous Caesar quote about ides is, "The ides of March have come." not exactly a blockbuster quote when compared to other stuff he said. For example, as every student of Latin knows, he said, "All Gaul is divided into three parts (Gallia est omnia divisa in partes tres)."

Translated into modern English, Julius was saying, "Gaul is all divided into parts three." Ancient Romans usually talked backward. What he meant was that Gaul was made up of France, Belgium and the Po Valley, probably a depressed economic area.

I can't imagine Caesar was saying this to the people in Gaul. Obviously they already knew they were divided into three parts.

Another thing Caesar said was, "Et tu Brute?" That was when he was about to be stabbed by Brutus and other ancient Romans.

Suetonius, also known as a boy named Sue, thought Caesar said these words in Greek.

So when Caesar yelled, "et tu Brute" to his fair-weather friend Brutus, maybe Brutus misunderstood.

Maybe Caesar said, "Your mother eats broccoli."

Maybe we are digressing.

You probably didn't know that the original Roman calendar put together in about the eighth century B.C. was only 10 months long, or 304 days. And it began on March 1. If we still used that calendar today, we could put April 15 somewhere in January or February, neither of which existed then. Because there would be no April 15, there would be no income tax.

King Numa Pompilius added January and February a little before 700 B.C. thus paving the way for the Internal Revenue Service.

England adopted the new Gregorian calendar in 1752. By then the Julian calendar was off by about 11 days. So the British, who like things orderly, on September 3 decided it was really September 14, thereby causing approximately a week and a half to vanish (like balancing your checkbook).

So don't try to tell me your birthday is September 4, 1752.

Anyway, the first day of the year went from March 25 to January 1. So, if not for the British, the worst hangover of the year would be on March 25.

CHEESE CAN BE MADE FROM THE MILK OF ZEBUS

SURELY YOU HAVE SEEN the commercials showing a chunk of cheese making jokes and a guy in a white coat saying the cheese isn't mature enough. The guy in the coat makes cheese crackers.

I don't think cheese can really talk, but if it could, it probably would say that it didn't matter because there wasn't enough cheese in a cracker to worry about.

There's so much other stuff in those little crackers that there is barely any room for cheese.

Cheese has been around for thousands of years and I have tried to eat as much of it as I can. My favorites are cheddar and Roquefort, a French cheese that was a favorite of Charlemagne. It's called the cheese of kings and popes.

All I know is that you know you are eating cheese when you bite into a hunk of Roquefort.

My granddad liked Limburger cheese. It's known for its odor, caused by the bacteria that is partially responsible for body odor.

My grandmother wouldn't allow it in the house, so he kept it in his shop down the hill from the house. Even mice that couldn't smell anything could find the Limburger, so he kept it in a covered bucket. He'd slip down the hill and cut off a chunk with his pocket knife, then eat an onion or an apple so he could get back in the house.

I had an experience with a French cheese smellier than Limburger.

When I was the agriculture writer for a Kansas newspaper I got a postcard outlining a contest for farm writers all over the country. It had pictures of cows, chickens and hogs, four of each. We were to rate the pictures on best meat, egg laying and milk production. The winner would get a free 12-month subscription to cheese-of-the month.

I won the contest and the cheeses began to arrive near the first of each month. I went on a two-week vacation and a cheese came in. It was a soft, French cheese more odorous than even Limburger.

People in the mail room began to smell something strange somewhere in a huge stack of mail. Each day as it permeated the cardboard box it got stronger.

In desperation, the mail room crew put the box in another box, stuffed newspapers around the inside box and sealed it.

The next day it was worse and they stuffed the two boxes into a third and sealed it. By the time I returned from vacation, the cheese was in four sealed boxes and the whole basement smelled like dirty socks.

To keep from smelling up our house, I ate the cheese.

Cheese begins as milk, blinky milk as my mother would have said.

A fellow journalist capitalized on that several years ago. He worked as an intern at the Rochester Times-Union.

This young fellow was assigned to write shorts. These are one or two paragraph stories that fill in where type doesn't quite complete a column. Newspapers try not to fill space with emptiness.

He got tired of finding these short pieces through research so he hit upon an ingenious way to manufacture shorts that were technically true.

He prepared a list of mammals, and at first wrote, "cheese can be made from the milk of zebus," then yaks or bison or bantengs. The list continued to goats, sheep and other milk producing animals.

He had a few mammals left on his list at the end of the summer, but a wily editor noticed a pattern. He admired the ingenuity but decided to end the cheese saga.

So no one knew until now that cheese could have been made from the milk of mastodons.

SOME FOLKS CAN'T RESIST THE URGE TO BARBECUE STUFF

THERE MAY BE a correlation between stupidity and barbecuing for some people. Why? Because I did it once and then did it again.

The first was when I was in the Air Force in San Antonio and my wife Dorothy worked at a radio station with live entertainers (as opposed to dead ones). It was about 1953.

The staff decided to have a picnic and needed a person to barbecue a modest number of chickens. Naturally, I volunteered.

I dug two holes and filled one with logs. Across the second one, I stretched chicken wire. Why chicken wire? I was barbecuing chickens.

The idea was to turn the logs into coals, then shovel them under the chickens. If it got too hot, I'd shovel some coals from under the chickens. I slathered on sauce and started shoveling. Too much heat. Shovel, shovel, shovel. Not enough heat—shovel shovel, shovel. Meanwhile, the chicken was black and kind of mummified. Smokey tears flowed down my cheeks. Before the chicken turned into charcoal, I announced that it was ready.

"Ready for what?" said someone.

"This chicken is burned," said Tony in the sonorous tones of an old-time radio announcer.

"You didn't want it raw, did you?"

They didn't want it either way.

Maybe we should just forget the chicken. But there were no pizza places in those days, so we ate deviled eggs and potato salad.

I didn't learn a lot from this fiasco. Several years later I worked at newspaper that had a recreation area called The Fourth Estate, and one hot, summer day the staff, including editorial, press room, composing room, advertising, 150 people or so, had a picnic.

Someone who could barbecue several crates of chickens was needed. Naturally, I volunteered myself and Dorothy. I dug two holes, only bigger ones. We had a really big hole for the chickens and a conflagration in the other one.

We turned the chickens with gloved hands soon caked in sauce and soot. People were hungry and they were grabbing chickens off the wire.

"This chicken is RAW," said one.

"This chicken is BURNED," said another.

They were right.

Tears were streaming down our cheeks. The picnickers were not happy. Dorothy and I were not happy. the chickens didn't look happy. I had visions of townspeople with torches and pitchforks yelling, "down with the chicken burners."

I had learned my lesson. Never again did I barbecue chickens for a large number of people. I barbecued hogs. I built a spit and invited a large group of people to help celebrate my birthday. We would buy a hog, impale it on a spit, build a fire and keep turning until it was done. What could be simpler? Not barbecuing a hog, I learned.

I sent Dorothy and one of our daughters to a town 50 miles north to buy the hog. They got lost and then got stuck on a muddy country road. They got back barely in time to get the hog on the spit.

They would have been there just in time if we had been able to get the hog on the spit. We couldn't because the farmer had sliced the hog in half down the spine. We couldn't think of a way to get half a hog on a spit.

So we wired the hog back together with baling wire and tied it on the spit. It kept falling off into the dirt. We brushed it off and pressed on.

We didn't burn the hog because we couldn't keep the fire going long enough. Luckily, it was dark by the time we took it off.

The guests praised the meat. After all, it was my birthday.

If you are planning a party and need someone to barbecue something, don't call me.

SOMETIMES AVOIDING CLUTTER IS ACTUALLY CLUTTERING

SINCE I WAS about 12 years old (quite a while ago) I have been trying to get organized. You know—hang my coat on the same hanger every time so that I will always know where it is when winter comes.

I always find it eventually, but it's often in the summer when I don't really need it. Sometimes I'm tempted to wear it anyway even if I sweat a little because I don't want to waste finding a garment.

I have bought books on how to manage time and how to make lists with priorities. I usually misplace the books. But I do keep a notebook (easily misplaced) with one item on the first page: "get organized."

Over the years I have pretty much decided to live with my disarray. Unfortunately, I haven't convinced my wife to live with it. She keeps nagging me about my messy office—just because she can't find her way to my desk (I'm sure it's still there).

My woodworking shop is kind of messy, too, but I figure that's good because I can't get through the debris to my saw. Obviously that's a safety feature. If I can't get to my saw, I can't cut off a finger—or a toe should I lose my balance.

One day I decided I'd had enough and set out to organize the shop. It would be a thing of beauty with everything in its place. I cut out a piece of wood and drilled holes in it to hold all of my screwdrivers. I couldn't find any screwdrivers. Next, I picked up all the wood scraps on the floor. I put them back. You never know when you'll need a small scrap of wood.

Next, I looked at all that sawdust on the floor and pretty much everywhere else. I turned on my shop vacuum but nothing happened because it wasn't plugged in. That was because all of the outlets had something plugged in. Some of the outlets are behind heavy machinery which doesn't matter because I can't get to the machines either.

I decided that if I wore a dust mask, I could just leave the dust—that is if I had a dust mask.

I did some research. I found that organizing "really comes down to automating decisions about where everything goes."

Well, duh! I've been doing that all along.

When I have an object I don't have a place for, I throw it in a pile in the corner. When the corner is full there still are three more.

Another tip I came across was to do away with duplication. "Why have two nonstick spatulas when one is enough?"

The answer is you need two because one is in the dishwasher, and a person who clutters does not turn on a dishwasher until nothing more can be crammed into it.

I almost forgot. You can't write a learned treatise without defining something. So here it is: the dictionary says that clutter is "to make disorderly or hard to use by filling or covering with objects."

By that definition, buying a plastic box at the department store to reduce clutter and filling it with objects that are cluttering your office or bedroom or kitchen actually is cluttering. And, if you cover the box with something to hide it, you are cluttering again.

So to avoid a mess, leave the stuff where it is. This is the way I have been dealing with clutter all my life. So what's the big deal?

WHAT EVER YOU DO
DON'T NAME YOUR COWS

THE OTHER DAY I was looking at the fences that enclose our 20 acres. Well, actually I was looking at the holes in the fences. Happily, I don't have to worry about that any more. Why? Because we don't have any cows.

There was a time when finding a hole in the fence meant I wouldn't find any cows, though some hapless motorist on the highway might.

Not long after we bought our property just north of the Rose Hill, a small town south of Wichita, I decided that a good way to keep the grass short was to buy some cows. They would eat the grass, then we would eat the cows, saving us the need to eat the grass.

It seemed like a good idea until we had named all six of the cows (technically they were heifers, not having been introduced to a gentleman cow). Shortly after we had named the heifers, the vet came over to give them some shots. The first thing he said was, "Don't name the cows."

It was a little too late. There was Hazel, Curious, Gentle, Little Cow, Brown Cow and another one I don't remember. The vet was right, of course, they had become pets and you don't usually eat your pets.

Getting into the cattle business was a natural. Back in the 1950s I had been a farm writer for a newspaper, so obviously I knew all I needed to know about cattle.

The fences on the place were designed to keep in sheep. And they don't seem to mind staying in the pasture as long as there is grass to eat. Soon after I had begun this adventure, my oldest daughter came home for Christmas. "Dad," she said with that all-knowing look, "you'd better get some barbed wire on those fences." She, too, knows all about the cattle business because she has lived in Wyoming.

I should tell you that Hazel was a really big cow, mostly Holstein. To make things worse, she had a mean look in her eye. She seemed to be telling me, "go ahead, put up barbed wire. It's not stopping me."

I put a strand around the top of the fences then she started rooting under the fence. I put a strand around the bottom. Hazel waited until it rained and the ground was soft then just walked over the fence.

At this point, chicken farming looked pretty good. Putting up chicken wire fences didn't appeal to me much, though.

A friend offered to let me keep his Angus bull for a time.

I took him up on it and wouldn't you know, the Heifers became cows. We were about to face another dilemma. If you can't eat a pet cow, how do you sell its calf?

Eventually our neighbor who knows a lot about cattle took them to the sale in Winfield. My wife Dorothy had to be restrained from running after the truck.

The next season we had another six calves, four of which were bulls. The vet came over, chased them all over the pasture and eventually made them into steers. The third batch was more of a problem.

We had four more bull calves. Under ideal conditions, they are made into steers when they are very young. They're easier to handle and they recover faster. We waited too long. The calves were the size of Great Danes. I called my neighbor for help.

"Do you have an enclosure?" he asked. I had a dog run which I learned is technically an enclosure but not exactly the right kind.

We got into the run with the four calves. My neighbor grabbed some legs from the abundance of them thrashing around and threw a calf on his side. "Sit on his neck," he yelled. "I'm not tall enough," I yelled.

I finally found what looked like a neck and sat on it. Big mistake. He threw me to the top of the dog run and scrambled to his feet. We tried another one. By then one of the mothers came over to see what dastardly things we were trying to do to her child. She tried to get in and the calves and I tried to get out. In 45 minutes or so (it seemed like 45 days) the deed was done.

Surprisingly, the neighbor still speaks to me. I saw the experience as an omen: "get out of the cattle business." I did.

IF YOU SHAVE WITH SHARK TEETH MAKE SURE THE SHARK IS DEAD

I HAVE BEEN USING an electric razor for several years now and the most important advantage is that I don't have to buy blades that cost as much as a steak dinner.

One of the disadvantages is that sometimes I can't tell whether I have actually shaved.

My granddad used a straight razor, and I can't remember that he ever cut himself. That's because he seldom shaved. Some barbers still use straight razors. They are scary-sharp instruments that could cut off a finger and you wouldn't know it for 10 minutes or so.

Pictures on cave walls show prehistoric people shaving with clamshells, flint knives and even shark teeth. Presumably, if the shark was alive, you would just let the whiskers grow.

Some historical accounts say the Roman King Lucius Tarquinius Priscus introduced the razor to his people in the 6th century BC, but shaving didn't catch on with Romans for another hundred years or so. The Romans probably figured that if they were going to get cut up, it didn't make much sense to do it themselves.

Men (and women) have been shaving for thousands of years, though the bearded look has come and gone with sideburns to match. Often men have gone for just a mustache, some bushy and others thin and fancy that go well with a cigarette in a holder.

I can't help admiring the facial adornment of men of the 19th century, but I can't get used to the five o'clock shadow look you see in the posh men's and women's magazines. It's common in catalogs, too.

Someone apparently thinks a day's growth of whiskers is sexy.

To me it means the guy was out late, has a hangover and his alarm didn't go off.

Meanwhile the companies that still make razors with blades are not giving up. They're staying afloat through innovation. Who would have thought anything could be done to make a safety razor different?

For years there was the single-blade razor that used a blade that has been relegated to scraping paint off of windows. The first big improvement was the double-edge razor. It used a blade sharp on both sides (all the better to slice your thumb off, my dear).

Now when sales slip, the razor companies just add another blade and charge accordingly. Some have as many as five blades. If a whisker survives the scraping of five (count 'em) blades, it deserves to live and become part of a sexy five o'clock shadow beard.

My dentist, who has black hair and whiskers to match, has adopted the shadow beard look. He told me (with his hand in my mouth so that I couldn't make any snide comments) that he had been dating and that someone told him the shadow beard was overwhelmingly sexy.

He didn't tell me whether it worked, but he's still wearing it and he smiles a lot .

The shadow beard or "designer stubble" as it is sometimes called made its mark in the mid-eighties when Don Johnson wore it on Miami Vice.

Kohl's puts out sales flyers that feature a guy with blond, wavy hair. He has a face full of blond designer stubble that doesn't show up very well. Maybe he should consider dyeing it a more fashionable dark brown.

I don't know whether you can buy five o'clock shadow dye. but if you can, I'm not going to buy any.

I like the electric razor because it doesn't cost much to operate and it's quick and easy. It's quick because it leaves a lot of whiskers intact, especially the ones around your lips. These are annoying because you can feel them and you know you missed them and everybody is looking at you and thinking, "HE uses an electric razor."

It's easy to use because you simply push a button and it buzzes into action—unless you forgot to put it on the charger.

At my age, I think I'll forgo designer stubble. Gray whiskers don't show up well and if I'm going to have hair, I want it on my head.

WHEN THE WIND COMES UP EVEN THERMOS WATER IS CHOPPY

TO THE SOUTH of our house is a garage that served the original owners of the farm our place is a part of. We use it to house two tractors and to store garden hoses and such.

Along the west wall gathering dust is the outboard motor once attached to our sail boat which mercifully was sold long ago. When no one is looking I kick the old motor. It makes me feel good and after all, you can't do anything to an outboard motor that will make it worse than it already is.

I have owned three boats in my life, the sailboat and two fishing boats. Each had an outboard motor, and a paddle to get us back when the motor quit. That would be when we took the boat out.

There is a rule governing outboard motors: They perform perfectly when placed in a barrel of water for testing, but will run only long enough to get you into deep water when attached to a boat.

Our first fishing boat was a bass boat, a flat-bottomed vessel more like a raft than a boat. Bass boats are made for still water (stagnant would be even better). It's fairly stable when tied to the dock but uncontrollable anywhere in open water.

I learned this a few years ago when we had the boat on Lake Cheney. One of the passengers was my nephew from Colorado. We were in a cove on the east side of the lake when the wind came up suddenly. When that happens at Cheney, there is no still water—even in your Thermos. The tops of the waves are as white as your knuckles when hanging onto the boat's nearest protuberance.

It occurred to me that my nephew, confined to a wheel chair, might have a problem if the boat sank. It occurred to me that the rest of us might also have a problem. Water was coming over the side and, as any good captain knows, if your boat is full of water, it will sink.

My task was to get out of the cove and back to the dock. Happily, the motor started. I decided to make good use of it before it quit, which would be very soon if experience meant anything.

The faster I went the higher the bow lifted above the waves. And, the less bow in the water the less control there was of the boat. I decided speed was preferable to caution and opened the throttle.

By then only the propeller was in the water. The boat was waving back and forth like windshield wipers in a downpour. To add to the excitement, there was a huge bump as the motor chewed through a submerged log.

I was terrified as were my passengers except for my nephew. He was having a great time yelling and gleefully waving his arms.

The dock was coming up fast and I began to wonder whether I would be able to stop my motorized barge. Luckily, another submerged log slowed us enough to eventually load the boat on the trailer.

I decided then that I would trade the bass boat for something with sides on it. I bought a tri-hull high enough to get us as far from the water as possible. It had a 40 HP motor that purred when we started it and got us out on the lake for fishing and even better—back to shore.

Then the outboard motor rule kicked in. There was a nice breeze (no whitecaps), it was overcast so the sun wasn't beating down and life was good. I opened the throttle so that the wind would blow though our hair, and the motor sputtered and quit. We paddled in.

A similar event occurred nearly every time we took the boat out—get to the middle of the lake, and sputter, sputter, sputter then silence.

We took the boat to at least two repair shops in Wichita and the motor ran in the barrel then quit on the lake. We took it to my uncle's favorite repairman in another town with the same result.

I parked the boat and decided to mutter and fume instead of risking another stall on the lake.

Then one day John, a friend from church, said he'd like to take a crack at it. He had the boat for a day or two and found a loose wire that interrupted the ground. He tightened a screw and the motor was fixed.

I sold the boat. Sooner or later another screw would work loose.

GERMS HIDE AND WAIT
TO GIVE YOU PNEUMONIA

WE FOUND A MATURE package of beef in the freezer, and being senior citizens, we popped it in the oven and later we ate it (the beef).

We have young friends—and relatives—who would be horrified. They would die suddenly if they were to eat any of it inadvertently. Out-dated food products are fatal to anyone 60 or younger.

That is why our young friends throw away all leftovers (is it really a leftover if it is thrown away)? In any case, you can't eat anything that has had time to cool. So, if it burns your mouth, that's the price of caution. I'm as fearful of germs as the next fellow. I don't touch the escalator railing even if I fall down and break a hip. I'd rather die of bone fracture than bacteria that like as not will devour my brain and most if not all my flesh.

I avoid rubbing my eyes because the consequences can be dire. I'm not talking about injury to the eye. I refer to germs—nasty, filthy microbes that lurk in places we don't talk about in polite society. Germs hide and gleefully wait to cause an unwanted case of pneumonia.

They're everywhere, and wouldn't you know it? You can't see them. You'd think that if they're bent on causing so much grief, they'd have the decency to show themselves and put up a fair fight.

But like it or not, germs have always been with us, though they were a lot less lethal when people didn't know they existed. If you were ill, you sent for the barber and had him let some of your blood out. If the wound got infected, you could get bled again (in a different place).

In their defense, surgeons did wash their hands, after the operation.

But let's get back to the freezer artifacts. We have a rule at our house: if it's more than two years old, we cook it longer.

When our son and daughter-in-law come over for breakfast, they check the sell-by date on the milk. If it's close, they drink water. They're adventurous enough that they don't boil the water.

I don't look at sell-by dates. If there is some left, it's drinkable.

Of course, they don't hesitate to put sour cream on a potato (not a left-over potato, of course). I hate to tell them that sour cream is made from—you guessed it—sour cream.

We have other ways of fighting germs, too. We wash our hands in liquid soap that will destroy germs even before contact.

We wash down the toilet with even stronger chemicals. You can tell they are strong because they are dyed blue.

My wife doesn't fear germs. She does not hesitate to eat an apple that has blown off of the tree and is buried in dirt. If there is a worm in it, he or she (or should I say he AND she) just have to get out of the way.

When I was a kid we visited the outhouse when absolutely necessary, and we were concerned with the wind blowing up under the seat in winter and the wasps, bees and spiders in summer. I'm sure the germs were there, too, but there was no fun in it for them because they didn't know they could hurt us.

But before I get a bunch of nasty letters, I want to point out that we should avoid germs. I'm just saying that it's possible to go overboard. We need a few germs just to keep our immune systems working.

When I grew up in the Great Depression the well pump outside my father's gas station had a tin cup attached to it with baling wire. Everyone used that cup. Apparently, people assumed that if it looked clean, it was clean. I'm happy the cup is gone.

I have read that in ancient days the sheets hardly ever were changed at roadside inns. If they looked reasonably clean they were left for the next guest. I imagine some folks slept on their horses. But eating an outdated pot roast probably didn't bother them a lot and it doesn't bother me that much either.

BORN WITH SHORT LEGS?
JUST WALK A LITTLE FASTER

REMEMBER THE MOVIE, "Honey, I Shrunk the Kids?" Neither do I, but I think somebody shrunk me. I went for my annual physical the other day and discovered I'm more than an inch shorter than I once was. I knew I wasn't 5 feet 6 inches as I claimed to be in high school, but 5 feet 3 inches? Come on. Kids these days are born taller than that.

When I was younger and applying for a driver's license I got measured with my shoes on. The idea was, I suppose, that most of the time when you were driving you would have shoes on. The nurse apparently thinks I walk around barefoot.

As my grown kids will attest, I have never gone anywhere (including to bed) without being properly shod. I want to die with my boots on, as they say, because I will be at least an inch taller

There's a reason for this getting-shorter problem. Both men and women get shorter after the age of 30. If I had known that, I would have skipped my 30th birthday. I don't have any height to squander.

Usually a man shrinks about 1 3/8 inches in his lifetime and women about two inches. The doctors say this is part of the natural aging process as the body loses muscle and fat. Well, I may have lost a muscle here and there, but fat? No way.

It's a dirty shame. As if getting old weren't enough, you have to get shorter, too. Worse, I was short to begin with. If one of the reasons is that I've lost some fat, why don't I get taller when I gain weight?

I hate to say this, but it's nice that women lose more height than men. It makes them easier to dance with.

Actually, it's not such a bad deal. I've always been short. It seems like I've always been the same size— a little smaller at birth, of course. I was taller than the other kids in grade school. Then at about the fifth grade, even some of the girls outgrew me.

Medical researchers say that people don't just shrink as they grow older, they also get shorter during the day. This is because water in the spinal discs is compressed by gravity while they're upright. So, to stay tall, sleep through the day and try not to walk upright.

By the next morning, your body has recovered and is back to its normal short height.

There are some disadvantages to being short. One is that trousers are made for normal people who are known in the clothing business as "regulars." You don't find many clothing stores that handle sport coats and suits in short sizes— unless the buyer is short. At this point I was going to outline the advantages of being short, I couldn't think of any. There's a bromide about short people being close to the ground and when they fall down it doesn't hurt them because they don't have far to fall. It doesn't really work. Falling down doesn't feel good at all.

Some famous people were short. Genghis Khan was 5 feet 1 inch, Mahatma Gandhi, 5 feet 3 inches; Pablo Picasso, 5 feet 4 inches, and Voltaire, 5 feet 3 inches. Napoleon Bonaparte supposedly was 5 feet 2 inches, but that was according to French measurement at the time. In terms of modern measure, he probably was 5 feet 6 or 7.

The French never get anything right.

We pretty much have to be thankful for what we are given. If we are born with short legs, we just have to walk fast. If we want to see over crowds, we have to bring a ladder. If we get hugged, we have to get used to regulars stooping over to do it.

The gas pedal is always too far away and when we move the seat forward our head touches the car's headliner. The people in front of us at the theater are always too tall to see around, you have to be on the front row in group photographs, no one chooses us to play on a basketball team, we never get to see a parade, and we have to endure the short jokes that taller people think are funny.

I've read that short people are more aggressive. It's called the Napoleon complex. It's not supported by any psychological studies, and I don't believe it. I have never been aggressive because I don't like the idea of getting punched in the nose by a taller person — or short person. So I've decided that if I have to get shorter to get older, I'm happy with that.

MAYFLIES DON'T EAT MUCH THEY DON'T HAVE A MOUTH

I OCCASIONALLY WATCH one of those fishing shows on TV and marvel at how easy they make it look. They cast a lure near a pile of brush and instead of hopelessly snagging the line they hook a near-record, large-mouth bass.

I try this and my lure hangs from a tree six feet above a pool of murky water that is free of fish. The more I yank, the tighter it gets. Finally I cut the line and look for another lure, possibly to snag on a sunken log.

This all began when I was about eight years old. I went with my parents, an uncle and my grandparents to Lake Taneycomo in Missouri. It's near Forsyth, a resort area. In the mid 1930s it was a village. We hired a teenager to guide us to a spot where we could seine for bait, the kind fish hate.

My granddad rented a boat that looked like a hog trough. It was made of wood that had seen better days. It was flat on the bottom and pretty much flat on both ends. It was not made for deep-water fishing. It was not made for shallow-water fishing. It would not have been safe on dry land.

We were told by the locals that the best bait was mayflies. These insects are about one and a quarter inches long and shorter in height. You have to catch them fast because they die in a day or so. These little flies were so numerous they covered everything including fishermen.

Our thinking was that they should be happy to die for a good-sized fish since they weren't going to live very long anyway.

Getting them on a hook was like threading a worm onto steel cable from the Golden Gate Bridge. Sometimes they died before you got them on. I could say they died like flies, but that would be a cheap joke.

My Uncle Elmer finally got one on his hook and he was so happy that he cast his line out with gusto. The hook, along with a dying mayfly got stuck in my ear lobe. Elmer cut the barb off with nippers and pulled the shank back through my ear. If it had been fashionable then, I could have worn it as an earring. I would have taken the mayfly off, of course.

We decided to try another fishing spot. We were near the middle of the lake when a large house boat went by.

Its wake nearly capsized our "boat." We were all too scared to scream. We fished from the bank for the rest of our trip and didn't catch any more fish than we did in the boat (none).

There is some good in everything, though. We learned something about mayflies, not that we particularly wanted to.

Mayflies spend a year awaiting birth, and when they're born they have but one purpose—to pass on their genes. They don't bother eating because one, they don't have time and two, they don't have a mouth.

Mayflies spend a whole year in freshwater in a nymph stage, in which they look a lot like adult mayflies. They don't actually do much during that year; they fly off to find a mate, lay some eggs and promptly die.

It hardly seems a worthwhile existence. You'd think that occasionally a nymph, bored with just hanging out would try to fly away early.

The problem with that is that there would be no mates around and the one day of debauchery would not happen. It would be enough to make a mayfly nymph want to become a larva and turn into a butterfly.

But with the luck of the average mayfly, a bird would come along and eat it. So, are there any advantages to being a mayfly?

The only one I can think of is that if you don't have a mouth, you don't have to worry about gaining weight.

DON'T ASK IF PROCRASTINATION IS RIGHT FOR YOU

LUCKY YOU, this column is about procrastination. I know what you are thinking: he's going to come up with a lame joke like, "I'm going to write a column about procrastination as soon as I get around to it."

There will be no cheap gags. We're serious.

So, before we get into the meat of the subject, let's define procrastination. Instead of jumping to the dictionary, which you could do yourself, we'll break the word down into its components.

You have your "pro" then you have your "cras" then "tin" and finally "ation." Anyone with a modicum (we'll do modicum in another column) of language training, will recognize pro as meaning, for example: "Let us consider the pros and cons." A "con", of course, is a person who has been in prison. A "pro" can also be someone who has been in prison, but usually is someone good at golf or some other sport.

"Cras" with an added "s" means crude and insensitive. Crass is from the Latin crassus, which we can ignore because Latin is a dead language and so is ol' Crassus.

Tin is an element—if you don't know what an element is, you aren't likely to find out here. Tin is used to make things of, such as tin cans. I am not going to get into a silly discussion about the fact that there is no "tin" in a tin can. There's no tin in the pasteboard can that Pringles come in either. Big deal.

So why call it a tin can? To confuse us even more, aluminum cans often are actually called tin cans. So why don't we just call the steel cans aluminum cans? I'm sorry to tell you that I just don't know.

There is some fuzziness about the makeup of metal cans. That's a sad kettle of fish (the kettle being aluminum). So we'll just drop the whole thing and get on with our subject if we can remember what it is.

We seem to have ignored the last part of procrastination, namely "ation." That comes from the word NATION minus the "N".

Now let's put it all together. A person who procrastinates is an uncouth, ex-con football player who eats string beans out of the can and doesn't know how to spell "nation". Now, was that so difficult?

So, how do we cure procrastination?

There is no pill for it, and if there were, the side effects would be horrendous. So don't ask your doctor if procrastination is right for you.

So what can we do?

Psychologists tell us we can beat procrastination if we prioritize. So let's break THAT into its components. You have your "pry" which means to move, lift or open something as with a crowbar. Then you have "or", which is a metal that can be mined profitably if you add an "e" at the end. "It" is usually a tiny pronoun but it can also be a noun. I'm having a problem with "ize". I could make sport of you and say that "ize" are what we see with, or maybe we could say it is frozen water.

Look it up in the dictionary and you find that to prioritize is to organize so that the most important thing is done or dealt with first.

With that in mind, I'm going to prioritize the writing of this column to show that I practice what I preach. I'm going to end it right now. And, not a moment too soon.

NEED AN IDEA?
PUT PAPER IN TYPEWRITER

I WAS GOING to say that countless readers have written to ask me how I come up with such fascinating topics for this column. I decided not to do that because no one has actually asked.

I could wait until someone did ask the question, but that could be a long time and I don't like to keep my readers waiting.

In the old days (a very long time ago) I told people that the best way to get an idea was to put a piece of paper in the typewriter and type something on it. You could only hope that the idea was one that concerned the subject for a column. Other kinds of ideas are okay, but are better suited to ways to fix a flat tire or some such thing.

I hasten to point out that ideas for fixing a flat are nothing to be sneezed at and of course can be filed away for future use.

I almost forgot about the piece of paper in the typewriter. I don't like to admit it, but this method of idea capturing has some flaws. One, it is difficult to find a typewriter these days and two, you have to come up with an idea to put on the blank sheet of paper.

The idea is to free associate. That's a psychological method developed in the 19th Century by Sigmund Freud. It goes like this: the patient is invited to relate whatever comes into his or her mind. Thoughts aren't to be censored. The technique is intended to help the patient learn more about what he or she thinks and feels.

We are not told why this is better than simply asking the patient how he or she thinks and feels. Be that as it may, we can let our mind come up with a thought, which we dutifully type on the paper. In the absence of a typewriter (almost a certainty), a computer and high-definition screen can be substituted.

So let us say that our thought is Clement Attlee! The exclamation point is not necessary but it adds a bit of panache.

Now, to free associate, we say the word, "panache" and see where it leads. It's a French word (already two strikes against it) that means a pleasingly flamboyant manner. That doesn't take us very far, does it?

It also means a flowery plume on the top of a soldier's hat. That is not much better, but "hat" rhymes with "cat" and that suggests a column about a cat in a hat. But that idea has already been discovered.

So it's back to the old drawing board or computer screen as it were.
It's possible that our first thought, Attlee! Was defective in some manner. I don't mean that Attlee! was defective, just the thought of him.

My advice is not to think of Clement Attlee! Write something anything on the paper.

I went back to some of my old books on writing to get ideas. Most of them said that you just have to start writing. They don't cover the concept that to start writing, you first have to have an idea.

So let's try again. Think. Think hard. Think harder. Any thought will do— except Attlee! He didn't work out so well. The thought is coming, coming, almost here. Shazzam! Geronimo.

There aren't many funny ideas coming from this thought. Geronimo was a pretty serious guy. He was an Apache warrior who fought the Mexican and the Texas armies. He probably didn't relate amusing anecdotes around the campfire.

So, we didn't come up with any column ideas, but most of us don't need to. But I've come up with a great one, Clement Attlee! I plan to put it in a folder and file it somewhere difficult to find.

THERE REALLY ISN'T ROOM FOR A GPS IN THE TOE OF A SOCK

WHEN I PUT on my socks the other day I noticed a small hole in the sole of one and an even smaller hole in the toe of the other.

I'm sure that many of you have more important problems. Well, to me, holes in my socks is a big problem. I don't like the feel of my bare foot in shoes. It feels clammy.

I have a friend who never wears socks. He wears penny loafers with his bare ankles out there for the world to see. Each to his own, I say, but really!! No socks?

My maternal grandfather was an oil field pumper and he wore farmer-type lace up shoes—without socks. He got out of bed each morning put on a blue Chambray shirt and blue denim overalls and stuck his feet into the shoes he left by the bedside. He didn't bother lacing them.

When I was growing up during the Great Depression, we didn't have a lot of money to buy new socks when they got holes in them. Someone darned them, usually my mother or my grandmother.

You never heard of darning? Well, lots of folks who had to do it wished they had never heard of it either.

It requires a special darning needle and a darning egg, usually made of wood, porcelain or metal. You could use a real egg, but if you squeeze it too hard, you will have a bigger problem than darning the sock. The work is done in an area that doesn't have a seam. If the hole is on a seam, you apparently are out of luck.

The darner (I'm not sure that's what you call them) sews across the hole in one direction, then weaves through these threads in a perpendicular direction. The result is almost like cloth, and often lasts longer than the sock. So you wear the holes while the rest of the sock just fades away.

But as I wrote earlier, darning has mostly disappeared—along with a large number of socks. A lot has been written (inadvisedly) about disappearing socks. For example, I hear they're making socks with GPS transmitters so you can track them down.

This is ludicrous because there isn't room in a sock for a foot and a GPS. Inventors need to think these things through.

And you know what happens when the techies invent an electronic gadget—they invent a bigger one that does even more.

You can see where the GPS in a sock is going. At first it will tell you where the sock is—say Bombay India. This will satisfy for a time, then the techies will find a new job for the sock, maybe a camera to take pictures of your feet. A spread sheet would tell you about your athlete's foot.

Even that will not be enough. If an electronic device works in a sock, why not put one in your pants? Then if you are about to sit on a sharp object, your pants would sound an alarm. Or if your pocket is being picked by an unscrupulous thief, a boxing glove on a stick would punch the crook in the nose.

Just make sure the electronic fist is turned toward the thief.

I think I deviated a bit. If you are old enough, you will remember that socks once were sold in sizes. Or, if you are old enough, maybe you won't remember much of anything.

Be that as it may socks now are manufactured in one size and if they are too small, you just pull harder when you put them on. If they are too big, you can wear them on the outside of your shoes.

When I was a kid, I often got socks for Christmas and my birthday. These socks were about as welcome as whooping cough. Now and then I got a tie, not a very popular gift either. What was a kid with holes in his socks going to do with a tie?

Socks then weren't very stretchy either. If you wore a size 10, that's what you'd better buy because you couldn't change them by stretching them. They were as pliable as aluminum and just about as comfortable.

The only consolation was that the shoes didn't fit very well either.

I DON'T THINK THE COMPUTER IN OUR REFRIGERATOR LIKES ME

THERE WAS A TIME when I could work on a car with some indication that it would actually start after the repair job. That was when I could get under the car—and get out from under it.

I have been known to replace fuel pumps, fix voltage regulators or generators, install new shock absorbers and clean and/or replace spark plugs. I even replaced the clutch on my daughter's Opal. Now it's hard to find a car with a clutch to replace.

The other day our stainless steel (we watch HGTV) refrigerator started freezing things—on the side that isn't supposed to freeze things. That side is supposed to stay at about 37 degrees F. Why 37 degrees and not 35 or 32? Apparently, it's the temperature the refrigerator's computer likes.

The other side, the deep freeze, stays at zero. That side wasn't affected by whatever malady had infected the machine.

The repairman didn't have to open the refrigerator door. He knew the problem was the computer. The remedy is to pull out the old one and put in a new $300 one. I know this because it has happened before.

Of course, he didn't have one. It had to be ordered from the high-priced refrigerator computer place. It took a week to get here and meanwhile, the refrigerator continued to freeze anything we put in it. Try making a salad with frozen lettuce. I'd like to send a plate of it to the CEO of the refrigerator company.

I shouldn't complain. The computer is necessary because it controls all the fancy features we don't want and doesn't work so well on the things we DO want.

It's called planned obsolescence.

I grew up in the oil fields and we didn't have refrigeration because we didn't have electricity. We didn't have running water either. We had only gas, and it came from a well nearby. The company let us use it because otherwise, it would have been flared. So, in about 1936, my dad bought an Electrolux-Servel refrigerator. It used a gas flame to expand the refrigerant and take the heat out of the box.

There were kerosene models, too. My wife's parents had one and it worked well, but made noises and filled the house with kerosene smell.

I was fascinated by the Electrolux' ability to make ice cubes.

We didn't have room for it in the two-room oil field shack, so we kept it in a shed. My mother had to walk outside to get eggs or milk but we never had to replace a computer. It's probably still working somewhere.

The more things our appliances do, the more quickly they quit doing them. That's why the stores want you to buy an extended warranty that costs nearly as much as the item it protects.

I'm still a little upset about the refrigerator. We've spent more than $600 on computers and I'm pretty sure the problem is a component like a resistor or capacitor that I could buy for 28 cents at Radio Shack. The problem is that I don't have the equipment to find the faulty component and I don't know for sure where it plugs into the refrigerator.

I think the new computer knows I don't like it because it doesn't keep the refrigerator at exactly 37 degrees any more. Now it fluctuates. Sometimes it's 37 and often 36 or 38—just enough variation to annoy.

If it didn't cost $300, I'd step on it.

SQUIRRELS ARE EXPERTS AT SAMPLING FRUIT

THIS IS A STORY about my life with squirrels. No, I was not an orphan in a tree raised by squirrels. That would be fascinating, but it didn't happen.

When I was a teenager living in Kansas oil fields I hunted squirrels. Occasionally, I shot one or two and my mother dressed them. No, she didn't put little frocks on them. She skinned them and soaked them in salted water before frying them. I'd like to say they tasted like chicken, but they didn't. They tasted like squirrels.

When I was 16 or so I developed a distaste for killing animals and I quit hunting. So over the years, considering my marksmanship, probably as many as four to six squirrels were spared.

That doesn't mean that I am fond of squirrels. They're rodents.

During the 23 years we lived in Wichita (we live out in the country south of the city now) we bought a lot north of our house and planted vegetables and several fruit trees.

Squirrels are nut eaters but they also eat fruit, and we had provided a squirrel smorgasbord. To say they eat fruit is not the whole story. They sample fruit. They take a bite from a peach, drop it and sample another, then another. In a while the ground is covered with sampled peaches.

I tried scaring them away, but my neighbor Charles fed them nuts. So there wasn't a lot of incentive to move out of the neighborhood.

One day my Uncle Elmer was visiting, and he spotted a squirrel in the peach tree sampling at a prodigious rate. We decided to scare him.

Elmer got on the west side of the tree and I on the east. Elmer yelled and clapped his hands while jumping up and down. The terrified squirrel dropped a peach and ran.

Now I was terrified. The squirrel ran straight at me. The animal was running for its life—toward what must have looked like a big tree stump to him. The squirrel seemed to get bigger as it approached.

It ran up my left arm, around my neck and down the right arm, leaving bleeding scratches on both arms. My uncle did not rush to my aid; he fell to the ground laughing. The rest of the family had been watching from a window of the house. They were rolling on the floor laughing. If squirrels laugh, they would have fallen out of a tree laughing.

At the time, I didn't see the humor. I had been attacked by a squirrel that not only was scared but also had been deprived of a peach.

That day I decided that no scrubby rodent would again terrify me. I would rid the neighborhood of squirrels.

I bought one of those traps that capture animals without hurting them. I baited it with a pecan and caught one the first day. I took the captive five miles north to a housing area I won't name because I'm sure it is by now infested with displaced squirrels. I relocated some 70 the first season and there appeared to be more squirrels than before.

I caught another 70 or so the next year, and still there were plenty of nervous squirrels for my neighbor to feed.

One day I set the trap with a nut and my wife and I went into town to do some shopping. It rained and when we got home we had caught a squirrel that had tried to escape during the downpour.

He had stirred up mud and debris trying to spring himself and was bedraggled. He was so tired he did not chatter—pretty unusual. I put the trap in the back of my Bronco and drove to the unnamed housing area.

Usually, when I freed them, the squirrels bounded out of the trap and hopped across the ditch delirious in their liberty. This one, however, just sat there and chattered.

He no doubt was telling me about the injustice of it all.

I turned the trap on end and shook him out. He walked slowly away, with his head held high, and he gave me an extremely dirty look.

THE WOODPECKER KNOWS
I HAVEN'T BOUGHT ANY SHELLS

I TAKE SOME PRIDE in calling myself an animal lover despite occasional annoyances. I can even understand Ben Franklin's choice of the turkey for our national emblem. But I'm pretty sure he wasn't referring to the wild turkeys that peck on windows.

Our house is partially underground on three sides, so the windows are at a handy beak height. And in spite of what you have heard about the size of turkey brains (about 2 percent of their body weight) they are among the most curious of birds.

So maybe they're just trying to see what's going on inside. They peck on the sliding doors on the north, then run to the west side and peck some more on the windows. This goes on for hours, before they quit to go chasing grasshoppers.

Sadly, a pesky redheaded woodpecker has picked up some pointers from the turkeys.

He's an obstinate bird who delights in landing on our windmill and pecking on the gear cover. The cover is mostly hollow and makes an excellent birdy bass drum. It's a dreadful noise that probably serves some woodpeckerly purpose but it does nothing for me.

It's loud and after 15 or 20 minutes of bang, bang, bang-bang, bangity bang, it gets mighty tiresome. I run toward the windmill flapping my arms and yelling, "go away" but the woodpecker just looks at me with those beady woodpecker eyes and keeps pecking.

Meanwhile, I'm thinking, no two-ounce bird is going to get the best of me. So I get the .22 rifle and wave it menacingly. The bird apparently senses that I haven't bought any ammunition since about 1950.

He seems to know, too, that shooting woodpeckers is against Federal law. I'll bet the guy who wrote that law didn't have a windmill.

The woodpecker just stares at me and goes on pecking. I run at him and he flies to a tree and waits. Then it's bang, bang, bang all over again.

That bird may think he has won, but this isn't my first rodeo. I have had other run-ins with animals. I wrote earlier about my bouts with squirrels. I have finally found a way to foil them. I don't plant fruit trees any more. I don't get any fruit, but neither do the squirrels.

I've also had a run-in or two with opossums. First, I'm not a fan of any animal that spells his or her name with an "O" in front of it.

It turns out though that possums and opossums aren't the same animal. Possums are part of some 80 species of marsupials that live mostly in Australia. Opossums represent about 100 species of marsupials that live in the Western hemisphere.

Marsupials are the mammals that include kangaroos, wallabies, koalas, wombats, Tasmanian devils, possums and opossums.

I'm wondering why anyone would call an animal a marsupial. As you probably know, marsupials usually have a pouch to house the little marsupials.

But as I mentioned above, I had a run-in with a opossum. He (as far as I know, it was a male) took up residence in one of Dorothy's big flower pots that had been dragged into the garage for the winter.

When I tell you this animal was big I mean it was HUGE, about the size of a bobcat. I have to admit that I have not actually measured a bob cat. But neither have I measured any opossums.

Anyway, the big opossum would not move from the flower pot. He adopted it as his home pot.

I tried the woodpecker ruse. I jumped up and down and flapped my arms, shouting "MOVE," Obviously, this was hopeless because I don't speak opossum and the opossum couldn't or chose not to speak English. I tried poking him with a yard stick.

The opossum's response was to show an array of very sharp teeth and to hiss at me. I have never heard of an attack opossum but I'm sure I had one. I was also pretty sure he wasn't going to leave any time soon.

I finally called the police and two officers came with a noose on a stick (a long stick) and arrested him.

I hope they took him to a flower pot far away.

I WASN'T JUST A CHUBBY KID
I WAS A ROUND LITTLE GUY

BEFORE I START writing the meat (an appropriate word as you will learn) of this column, I'm going to admit that when I was a kid I was chubby. Well, maybe not exactly chubby. I was FAT.

I was a round little guy who didn't run very fast. I didn't walk very fast either. Other kids weren't always kind to me, their fatso friend. They laughed at the clumsy way I played ring around the rosie.

I was a kid of the Great Depression, a time when parents usually had only one child. Many couples didn't have jobs and couldn't afford a larger family. So, they doted on their one offspring. In my family, I always got the extra pork chop or the leftover steak gravy.

It was the only-child pork—er perk.

Being fat was sort of a handicap. I was different. It carried through elementary school and junior high. I had to be forced to participate in sports. Because I wasn't very good at it, I avoided it and therefor was laughable on the playground. When I swung the bat there was a good deal of air between the bat and the ball. That wasn't so bad, because if you don't hit, you don't have to run.

The junior high coach thought I ought to play football. He reasoned that because I was heavy, I would make a good tackle. I knew enough about football to know that if you tackled someone, you had to run fast enough to catch him. And, if you made the tackle, you both fell down "hard". And, you stood the chance of getting hit yourself, and that would hurt.

The coach called me a sissy. I decided to accept that appellation as an alternative to playing football.

There were other disadvantages to being "fluffy". One was girls. I hasten to add that girls are not a disadvantage. Being fat is a disadvantage in terms of attracting them..

Another problem for fat boys is that they can't slip up on anyone while wearing corduroy pants because their thighs rub together.

And, when fat boys grow up a little they start having other problems with clothing. It's too small in inconvenient places.

Not only was I fat, I was short and fat.

That combination resulted in a kind of ball shape.

I never wanted to fall down near a hill because I'd roll to the bottom.

The legs of all the pants I bought had to be cut off, and because pants are always made for taller people, the cutoff was at about the knee. Thus the pant leg was shaped like the exhaust funnel of a steam boat—the same diameter at the top as at the bottom.

My parents weren't too concerned about my heaviness. If I had been born in the 1970s instead of the 1920s, we would have counted calories. Later in life I learned that counting calories is not a big problem. Eating things that contain them is the problem.

Thankfully, the fat problem resolved itself. When I was 11 years old I worked for a bachelor farmer who baled hay all summer long. His farm was about two miles west of our oil field shack.

World War II was on and he hired me because no one else was available. He paid me $2 a day to help him bale prairie hay and alfalfa. He used a stationary baler. That is one that stays in one place while you bring the hay to it.

He cut the grass with a sickle on his tractor. When it was dry enough I raked it into windrows with a team of horses. We started at sunrise.

Later I hitched a buck rake to the team and scooped up the hay, took it to the baler, then backed the horses up, releasing the hay.

The farmer pitched it into the baler's hopper and I did the rest—poked wires, tied them, put the wooden dividers in to set the size of the bales, and stacked them when they came out. I was doing the work of a three-man crew and he was pitching all day long. Temperatures were at 100 or near it a good deal of the time.

When it got dark we loaded the bales into the barn loft.

The fat melted away and most of it did not return. Yipeee!!

YOUR BOSS HAS GREAT IDEAS BUT YOU MAY NOT LIKE THEM

NOW AND THEN people ask me how I get ideas. They will say something like, "How do you get ideas for your articles?"

I reply, "They aren't articles; they're columns."

"They look like articles to me."

The way most newspaper people get ideas for "articles" is to go to the city desk and the city editor says something like, "Go cover the undertaker's convention." That's a wonderful idea because the editor says it is.

Just to keep things straight, an article is a story about something that happened, and is called straight news. A feature article is factual but it's about something that is interesting though not necessarily a news event. An editorial is opinion and is displayed on the editorial page. A column can be opinion or a personal story that can be part fiction. A column is an essay.

But let's get back to ideas. First we have to know what an idea is. James Webb Young, who wrote a book on the subject, said, "An idea is nothing more nor less than a new combination of old elements."

Phosphorus and oxygen aren't any older than other elements, but if you combine them, you're going to get a nasty explosion. So let's not do that. Young apparently had a problem getting ideas for books.

The dictionary has about four inches of words that try to define ideas. An example: "What exists in the mind as a presentation (as of something comprehended)". No wonder people have trouble getting ideas. No one knows what they are.

There are lots of books about getting ideas. They're pretty much alike, so I'll tell you what's in them and save you the cost of the books. I will give you only one or two methods because I may want to write a book some day and I don't want to give away all the good stuff.

First, most of the books say you need to know exactly which idea you want before you try to get it. In my case that would be an idea for a column. I already knew that before I read the book

I think they mean that I need to define the problem.

In that case, I would say, "I need an idea to keep me from losing my job." The next thing the books tell you is to do some research and go to bed. According to the books, your sub conscious mind will work on the problem and you will have an idea when you wake up.

So, I decided to try it. I did the research (mostly on things unrelated to the problem) and ate some leftovers, then went to bed. It worked. I awakened the next morning and an idea was waiting for me. I ran to the computer and wrote it down: "I'm hungry."

That wasn't the idea I was hoping for.

A few years ago brain storming was the rage. Note to TV weather people: brain storming is nothing to get excited about.

The rules are simple. You get a group of people together, preferably folks who have never had an idea in their lives. A person who doesn't like to think is put in the middle and becomes the interlocutor. That person is there to keep things going. That's needed because after an idea or two, things slow down and there is total silence—maybe some snoring.

Participants blurt out anything that comes to mind no matter how ridiculous. And, the rules say you can't judge any of the ideas—just keep 'em coming.

So it goes something like this: "Turn it upside down. Make it smaller. Put wheels on it and fold it up like a newspaper. Spread toothpaste on it."

It's difficult to keep from judging these kinds of ideas, but who knows? If Edison had spread toothpaste on the light bulb, there would have been less light coming through, but the moths might have had fewer cavities.

ONLY THE OLD GUYS CARRY POCKET KNIVES

ON MY LAST BIRTHDAY I was treated to a wiener roast at our son's house. He had gathered branches that had to be made into wiener sticks.

He asked whether anyone had a knife. His father-in-law and I, both in our 80s, each had one.

In my day (a far distant one) six-year-old boys had knives. Otherwise, they wouldn't have been able to cut fish bait or string for a kite.

In those days we were allowed to slice open a thumb now and then or close a blade on a finger or two. It was part of growing up.

We were told to be careful and not to run with an open knife. And we were advised not to cut a stick with the knife pointed toward us. That was to avoid opening an embarrassing hole in the stomach or some other organ.

We were trusted with all kinds of sharp objects, including single-edge razor blades. We didn't shave with them; we used them to cut balsa wood sticks that were part of the 10-cent model airplane kits we bought at the dime store.

I still have a scar on my left thumb acquired when I was trimming the sprue from a lead soldier. We were allowed to pour molten lead into these molds. They were cast iron to be bolted together for the pour and separated to get the soldier out (often before the mold had cooled).

I grew up in the oil fields and toy soldier material was readily available in the form of babbitt, an alloy usually containing tin, lead and copper. It was used for bearings in large machinery.

We melted the babbitt in a coffee can that had been bent on one end to resemble a pitcher. If the molten metal had spattered, we could have suffered eye damage or any number of serious body burns.

We learned to be careful but there were injuries. Nevertheless, my boyhood friends and I would have been mortified to be caught without a bone-handled, Sears folding pocket knife. A smaller model might have served but would have been considered wimpy.

As for razor blades, the single edge became obsolete because the double-edge razor was invented. The blade was thinner and sharp on two sides. To use it to assemble model airplanes, you broke it into two pieces.

Sometimes we forgot which side of the half-blade was sharp and sliced a finger or two.

I still carry a pocket knife. It's painful when I have to leave it at home when I board an airplane. I would sign an agreement with the government that I would not highjack the plane if they would let me keep my knife.

My granddad carried a pocket knife, and he used it for everything. He could peel an apple into a circular peel that looked like a slinky.

Knives were good for playing Mumbley peg, too. It was popular in the 19th century. It required two players who had to stick the knife in the ground using up to 24 different trick holds. The first to complete them could drive a stick into the ground with the handle of his knife.

The loser pulled the stick out with his teeth. The game was about as wild as boy parties got then. They didn't have computer games.

YOU DRIVE A PICKUP TRUCK TO KEEP THE CAR CLEAN

MY WIFE AND I agree on a lot of things but we don't see pickup trucks in the same light. For me, you drive a pickup to keep the other car clean. To her, a pickup is something you haul stuff in. Heavy and dirty stuff.

Now, I'm not averse to placing a small parcel in the middle of the pickup bed as long as it doesn't bounce around and scratch the paint.

Dorothy believes that if it will fit in the pickup—even partially—you can haul it somewhere. This worked pretty well with our old pickup, a 93 model. It had so many lumps and scratches you could acquire new ones and not be able to find them the next day.

To her, the weight capacity is whatever fits in the truck. That includes rocks (read boulders). She starts putting smaller rocks in when the bed touches the axle. She stops just before the springs break.

I bought a trailer so that limbs and yard debris could be hauled to recycling without scratching the pickup. So she fills the trailer then puts the rest—the ones with the most thorns—in the truck.

"You're scratching the paint," I tell her.

"Don't worry, it will rub out," she replies.

Of course it will rub out with sandpaper.

Dorothy thinks a pickup is like an off-road vehicle. You go where the junk is and you load it up and you haul it away. If you run over hedge tree thorns or off of a cliff, you don't go that way the next time. After all, pickups can be repaired.

Dorothy learned about pickups from her father who was a farmer and rancher in South Texas. He had a faded green 1964 GMC pickup. He drove it wherever he needed to be—through the sand dunes, over the caliche gravel roads and across plowed ground if necessary.

When I could work up the nerve, I rode with him. I noticed that when he pushed the brake pedal down, nothing happened. The truck moved at the same speed, then coasted to a stop (most of the time). "What's wrong with the brakes?" I asked.

"Nothing. I keep 'em loose because the sand gets in the linings and wears 'em out".

That's logical. If the brake linings wear out, you have to buy new ones. If they don't rub on anything, they won't wear out.

I figured it was a Texas thing and never brought it up again. I didn't ride with him any more either.

Farmers grow up with pickups and combines and tractors. They start driving everything from about age 7 or so. There's not a lot of traffic on the farm, so the kids don't run into many things.

When our son Tedd was about that age he was in Texas with his granddad, who was feeding cattle. He threw off some bales of hay and told Tedd to drive the pickup over. It was parked in a plowed milo field.

"But Granddad, I can't drive".

"What do you mean, you can't drive? What do they teach kids up there in Kansas? You're almost 8 and you can't drive a pickup"? He was probably thinking, "Next thing, he'll tell me he can't shoot a gun."

We recently traded the '93 pickup for a Ford Ranger. I have no idea why the company doesn't make Rangers any more. It's just right for people like us with some acreage but not enough for a real farm.

It gets pretty good gas mileage because it has a four-cylinder engine and it's not very heavy (unless Dorothy insists on hauling something in it). In other ways, it can be a bit weird.

I was repairing a door in the garage not long ago when I heard something that sounded like a car starting. But before I could investigate, it quit. Then it started again and it sounded like the pickup had started itself.

I opened the door and sure enough, the Ranger was running. There was no key in the ignition, so I couldn't find a way to shut it down. I went into the house for the keys and discovered Dorothy digging around in her purse. She had pushed a button on the key that remotely started the pickup. I didn't know it had a remote starting system.

The next time I buy a pickup I'll get one that lets ME decide when it gets started.

TYING YOUR SHOES
NOT AS EASY AS IT LOOKS

THE OTHER DAY I was tying my shoes and I got to thinking about the way I do it. I've been doing it the same way all my life. I think my Dad taught me, but I've noticed that some people arrive at the same destination in slightly different ways.

It's difficult to explain in writing, but I looked it up on the Internet and there are three ways of tying your shoes. One is called the circle technique. I'm sure I could never master it. My only alternative would be to let the laces flop or wear loafers that don't have shoe laces.

The second is the magic fingers. Unfortunately, I was not born with "magic" fingers or even "deceptive" fingers. I might have magic toes, but it would be difficult to tie my shoes with my toes because I would have to remove them from my shoes to get at the laces. That would seem to defeat the purpose.

The third method is the bunny ears technique. As near as I can tell, that's the one I use. It involves pulling up a loop and holding it with a finger while you wrap a second loop around that one and pull it tight (don't try this at home). I hold the first loop with my thumb, but it should qualify.

With all of these methods you must be careful not to tie your shoes together because that would make it difficult to walk and nearly impossible to run.

I think that pretty well exhausts the topic, but as you have no doubt discovered, one stupid observation often leads to another. For example the knotting of shoe laces makes me wonder about our other habitual endeavors. This could lead to a scientific thesis if I'm not careful.

But let's press on. How do you put your coat on? We wouldn't do that in this kind of weather of course, but this is a hypothetical

I've seen people hike the coat over their heads with their arms held upward to let the coat slide down. This works well for some people and if you are held up while putting on your coat, your hands are already in the air, saving time for you and the robber.

Others put an arm in one sleeve at a time then wiggle their shoulders. That's my method and it has worked for me. If you found a way to get the coat zipped up, the time will come when you have to get it off again.

Some people unzip, then hang both arms downward.

Then they let the coat drop. This is the lazy person's method. It takes less effort but results in a coat on the floor that has to be picked up.

I'm with the group that takes one arm out at a time while grabbing the collar before it falls to the floor.

This got me to thinking about Napoleon's portrait that shows him with a hand inside his coat. People have wondered why he had his hand in there. Don't scoff. Everybody has to wonder about SOMETHING.

Theories abound. Did he have a stomach ulcer or an itchy skin? Was he winding his watch, or was the artist a little shaky at painting hands?

The probable answer is that in the 18th century, painting a person with his hand in his or her coat was the in thing. It was like contemporary portraits that have people with an index finger up against the cheek. It was just a fad—a bad fad if I may say so.

Now comes the intriguing matter. How do you take your pants off. If you ask me, it's better to leave them on. You've heard the cliche about pants: "He puts his pants on one leg at a time." That's a bit silly especially if a person is standing. If that person tries to put the pants on both legs at once, that person will fall down.

So how do you get up when you fall down? Do you push up with an elbow? Roll over and get your hands under you? Or do you just go to sleep and worry about it in the morning?

It's something to think about. But not for long.

;

SALTWATER CATFISH ARE GOOD IF YOU'VE HAD A FEW CORONAS

THE GREAT THING about writing a column is that you can write about anything—and by the time you are reading it the deed has been done and there is nothing anyone can do about it. It's a power thing.

So, I'm going to write about catfish.

Why would anyone want to do that? Because I have run out of ideas and when you really need an idea, catfish are as good as any.

So that just about wraps it up. I'm joshing. There are tons to write about catfish and what I write, you certainly aren't going to find anywhere else.

To begin, let's try to answer the enigma of South Texans and saltwater catfish. My wife Dorothy is from South Texas so over the past 65 years or so we have visited there many times and have fished in the Gulf of Mexico.

I have been eating catfish as long as I can remember. My mother cleaned the bullheads I caught in farm ponds and fried them for me. They tasted a little muddy, but they were sort of edible.

Later I caught channel cat in Kansas lakes and they were delicious.

So I was surprised to discover that South Texans do not eat saltwater catfish. In fact when Texans catch one they say words that would make a Kansan blush then they toss them on the bank to die (the catfish, not the Kansans–usually) and be carted off by a javelina hog or some other critter. Texans call these fish "tourist trout."

They say saltwater catfish are bottom feeders, and that's usually the end of it. So you're left thinking a saltwater catfish is a vulture with gills.

Saltwater catfish do feed on sandy bottoms but they eat mostly live fish, mollusks and crabs along with algae and other plant material.

What the Texans probably are really complaining about is that saltwater catfish are slimy and hard to clean, and their fins are sharp and can inflict a painful puncture wound.

There are generally two kinds of these fish in the gulf, the hardhead catfish and the gafftopsail. The hardhead has a hard head (duh), that is, a bony plate that extends from the eyes to the dorsal fin. Getting through this while trying to hang on to a very slimy fish apparently is not something a South Texan wants to be bothered with.

The gafftopsail has a dorsal fin that looks like a sail on a boat (if you have had a few Coronas). Both fish are edible despite what Texans say.

55

Tests have been done that indicate people given a bite of fresh water catfish and saltwater fish can't tell the difference. Maybe that's because of the Coronas.

If you catch one of these fish, you need to handle it carefully. The spines contain a mild toxin. I know this because I have seen it in action.

My wife and I were fishing with her brother and a cousin at a place on the Rio Grande River where it empties into the Gulf of Mexico. Dorothy's cousin caught a large saltwater catfish and was not happy.

She reluctantly grabbed the slimy, slithering fish and with a look of disgust got the hook out. The fish, which weighed eight to ten pounds, flopped around on the dock and generally made a nuisance of itself.

She decided to toss it onto the bank like any good Texan, but stomped on it first. She was wearing sneakers and the dorsal fin went through the sole and into her foot. She screamed, shouted some unladylike Texas cuss words, and hopped around, making things worse.

We pulled the fish off of her foot and later a red streak went up her leg. We took her to a hospital.

So even if you don't like salt water catfish, don't step on any.

CLOTHING CAN BE UNSIGHTLY BUT IT COVERS UGLIER STUFF

HAVE YOU EVER noticed that as you get older your association with your clothes changes? Maybe I need to explain that. Well, you don't wear the same clothing you did a few years ago because 1. It probably needs laundering. 2. It doesn't fit any more. 3. You may not be as fashionable as you once were.

When I was a kid I wore striped overalls, the kind with the large stripes. I looked like a featherbed with legs—short legs. For you youngsters (anyone 65 or under) a featherbed is kind of an uber-mattress made of the same material as striped overalls and filled with goose feathers.

No one ever tells you why a goose would let you have enough feathers to make one of these. My grandmother had a featherbed on every bed and when I stayed at her house overnight, I disappeared in them. My other grandmother had a goose (gander type) that did not like me—or anyone else except maybe a female goose.

He chased me all over the yard nipping at my striped overalls and whatever was beneath them.

Later I wore corduroy pants (if you are an English major, you might wonder what happened to the transition). The Great Depression was on and my mother chose this fabric because it was cheap and never wore out. You could buy corduroy pants when you were 8 and wear them until you could vote in a presidential election.

Also my mom always knew where I was because she could hear me walking—swish, swash, swish etc. Anyone wearing corduroy could not hide fat thighs. It was like wearing a big neon sign that flashed, "This guy is chubby, this guy is chubby, this guy is chubby."

Another advantage was that you didn't have to iron corduroy. What good is a crease in your pants if you can't see it? I once owned a suit made entirely of corduroy. It easily doubled the swishing and swashing and you never had to pay a dry cleaning bill. You just threw it in the washer and later wished you hadn't because it shrank to the point of non-wearability (if that is a word).

Corduroy's earliest ancestor was a cotton cloth called "fustian" developed in the ancient Egyptian city of Fustat in 200 BC.

Some of the pants made by Fustat tailors are still being worn.

57

Historians say England's King Henry VIII was fond of corduroy. They don't say why.

There are other clothing anomalies (don't tell me you don't learn things from this column). I have put together some clothing rules:

1. New shoe laces will always be too short. Oh, you can tie them but there never is enough left to make a bow, so you just tie a granny knot, and you will be sleeping in those shoes.

2. The little buttons that fasten your collar tips to the front of your shirt cannot be unbuttoned, and if they somehow could unbutton themselves, you could not rebutton them. If you buy a shirt with these already buttoned, you will have to thread your tie through the collar.

3. You will always thread your tie through the wrong way.

4. When you get your tie through the buttoned collar—the right way— and you get it tied, the little end will be longer than the big end.

5. After you take it out and rethread it so the two ends are the same length, you will discover that you wanted a Windsor knot instead of a four-in-hand.

While we are delving into the mysteries of clothing, I want to quash the old wives' tale about missing socks. I am here to tell you that socks do not disappear. They multiply. I can't remember how many times I have found three of one kind of sock in my drawer.

As mysterious as that is, it is even more confounding that I did not buy any of these socks. They materialized spontaneously. You may think there is a reasonable explanation. I believe that aliens, intent on abducting me in my sleep got scared by the cat and left the socks just to play with my mind. If you can disprove this theory, be my guest.

Enough about my socks. Let's mention unmentionables. I should have mentioned this in my rules above, but better late than never. The elastic in underwear is not elastic. The dictionary defines elastic as "able to return to an original shape or size after being stretched or squeezed."

I have never thought of squeezing my shorts but I do stretch them (actually, I REALLY stretch them) and hardly ever do they return to their original shape. What once was the elastic now just hangs there and does not even try to do its job.

Nevertheless, clothing is necessary. As unsightly as it can be, it covers what can be even uglier.

COWS LIKE IT A LOT BETTER ON OTHER SIDE OF THE FENCE

WHEN WE HAD COWS on our 20 acres one of the first things I learned was to make fences. Unfortunately, I didn't learn to make fences that kept cows in. In the process, I learned one thing. That is that cows dearly love to be on the side of the fence you don't want them on.

I also learned that there is a good deal of difference between a little bit of chicken wire stretched around some tee-posts to keep the rabbits out of the garden and field fence for cattle. The difference is that the chicken wire will keep the rabbits out but the field fence usually won't keep determined cattle in.

Before the cows, I hadn't thought much about fencing. I could take it or leave it. With what I know now, I think I should have left it.

A few years earlier we planted a big garden. The rabbits were happy. I would have to build a fence.

I neglected to study the art of fencing. I told myself that building a fence is not rocket science. You unroll some fencing, drive some corner posts (at each of the four corners, of course), drive some tee-posts in between and stretch some wire over them.

What could be simpler. Almost anything, I learned.

First, you don't drive corner posts. You dig holes in the ground and put the posts in the holes, then you tamp the earth around them. Then you notice that the holes you dug were not perpendicular. But if you crook your head to the side and squint a little, they look almost upright.

I knew there would be some tension on the corner posts and they would have to be strong. So I braced them with some short little sticks nailed to the posts. As it turned out, this plan was flawed. I unrolled the woven wire fencing (which kept trying to roll itself back up) and fastened it to the corner posts.

I attached a come-along—a small, portable winch—(no, I didn't mean wench) and cranked until the wire fence looked pretty good. One more click would be perfection. I pulled the lever and all four posts came flying out of the ground, tangling the wire as they flew. The rabbits would have a hard time finding the lettuce.

That's when I looked at some fences. A corner post, I learned, is really three vertical posts and two horizontal posts.

59

I was so happy to learn these things that when we got cows at our place I decided to build some more ranching stuff. I got plans from the Kansas Department of Agriculture to build a squeeze chute. Its purpose was to squeeze cattle. Duh! Why would you want to do that?

Well, because you want the cow to stand still while the vet gives her a shot. Cattle are like people when it comes to shots. They don't like them. And, unless it involves cow feed, cows don't much like people to get close to them. If you do, they usually run or just step on your foot.

I was proud of the chute. It had a place for the cows to enter and at the other end was the "squeezer," two upright two-by-fours each bolted to the chute at the bottom. A piece of pipe was attached at the top as a lever to pull the two boards together and squeeze the cow's neck. A spring pulled the boards apart after the shot was administered.

I knew that something was wrong when the cows started turning around in the chute and going back out of the entrance. The vet holding the needle sensed that something was wrong, too.

The cows were probably thinking, "If anyone is going to get a shot, it's going to be the idiot who built this thing. We're out of here."

I had either built the chute too wide, or the cows weren't nearly fat enough. The posts holding the contraption together were four feet into the ground and not easily pulled out. I decided that chasing the cows was easier. And I simply abandoned the chute.

The next time shots were in order I borrowed my neighbor's portable squeeze chute. It kept the cows in line. The chute I built still stands after more than a decade. It didn't get a lot of wear and tear.

If you have any elephants—preferably fat ones— that need shots, I have a squeeze chute that just might work.

AN UMLAUT CAN HELP
REDUCE PAIN OF LEG CRAMP

WHAT'S THE MATTER with this guy? Does he think getting hurt is funny? I know it's not your problem, but writing a column that is supposed to be funny, well maybe mildly amusing, or at least not too heavy gets difficult. Sometimes I just can't come up with anything. Then one day in desperation, I thought, why not write about pain?

You're probably thinking pain is something to laugh about?

Have you ever watched a Laurel and Hardy movie? They drive their car into a ditch and it is demolished or one of them trips on something or a piano drops on them—all painful, and everyone laughs.

Here's a personal example:

I was installing guttering and downspouts on a shed. I was on a teetering ladder with a pocket full of nails and a hammer. Things went well for a while then a wasp came close as I was swinging the hammer. I missed the nail and hit my thumb.

I don't often swear but some pretty nasty words escaped before I could stop them. I threw the hammer hoping it would land on the wasp.

What could I do? It hurt. If I had had a little more time, maybe I could have come up with a more suitable outcry. I could have used the symbols the comics artists use to denote swear words.

When I hit my thumb I could have waved my arms wildly and yelled, "POUND SIGN! AMPERSAND!! PERCENT SIGN!!" I could even have shouted, "UMLAUT" but those two little dots don't show up very well.

Some people grab the injured member with the other hand and hold it while hopping around on one foot. Unfortunately this doesn't work well on a ladder. Others put the hurt finger or thumb in their mouth. I don't recommend this if you are wearing gloves.

You could also hold the hammer in both hands, then it would be impossible to hit your thumb. It would also be impossible to get the nails out of your pocket or hold on to the ladder.

Another personal example involves installing skirting on my daughter's mobile home that she lived in while she was in college.

This time it was a bunch of tools piled near the bathroom door.

I got up in the middle of the night and didn't bother to turn a light on. Naturally, I stubbed my toe on the pile of tools.

My first impulse was to grab the toe and hop around wildly, shouting pound signs and umlauts, but I couldn't remember any of them. I fell back on the tried and true ordinary swear words. That made me feel better but didn't do anything for my toe.

I took two aspirins then another one and went back to bed. The next morning my foot was swollen and wouldn't fit in my shoe. It hurt, too, but not the swearing kind of hurt

There is only one thing that hurts more than a stubbed toe and that is a muscle cramp. I usually get these in bed, particularly when I haven't had enough water or I have been on my feet a lot.

I get them in my feet and calves. I stretch and the pain strikes.

I am afraid to move because if I move, it will hurt even more. I know I have to get out of bed and walk to get rid of the pain, but walking is painful, too. So I just lie there hoping no one jiggles the bed.

Maybe I could smash a toe with the hammer. It would hurt, but it would take my mind off of the cramp.

Another funny pain is when I walk down to the road to get the morning paper and a tiny rock gets in a sandal. There is nowhere to sit down and remove it so I walk on it until I get back to the house.

I sit down to take off the sandal and the pebble has disappeared. I don't know whether to laugh or shout AMPERSAND, UMLAUT.

IT'S HARD FOR FISH TO SWIM
WHEN THE WATER'S FROZEN

LOOKING FOR A PET? You can't go far wrong with a goldfish. You could have a couple hundred of them and carry them in a bowling ball bag. You'd be wise to hurry when you do this because bowling bags are notorious leakers.

Goldfish make good pets because they don't bark or scratch the furniture and you can feed them for months from a package the size of tennis ball container.

You don't know how big a tennis ball container is? It's a lot smaller than a 50-pound sack of dog food. Goldfish don't do tricks, but they can be colorful and they swim well.

I hate to say this, but if I were a goldfish, I'd swim as far as I could from my wife Dorothy. She has a spotty relationship with these fish.

Dorothy was born near Hargill, TX, and that's about as far south as you can get without ending up in Mexico. She lived much of her life on a farm near Edinburg, TX. I'm pretty sure her dad would have complained about using water the cattle could drink to provide a pool for a bunch of goldfish.

So it wasn't until after we were married and had moved to Lawrence, KS that Dorothy acquired her first bowl of goldfish.

Having lived all of her life in the Rio Grande Valley, she had never seen snow and was not very familiar with temperatures below 40 degrees. It was 1954 and she worked in the Kansas University alumni office and I attended classes at the Journalism School.

Dorothy decided that her fish would be more robust if they got a lot of fresh air. It worked pretty well for people, she reasoned. So, she put the bowl of fish on the window sill and left the window open.

When we returned in the late afternoon the fish had acquired too much of a good thing. They were frozen solid. We bought more fish and let them breathe the ambient air that was in the water..

We have had myriad cats and dogs in the years since but until recently, no goldfish. Dorothy decided to try again. We bought three stock tanks.

We buried them a foot deep in the ground.

Then we filled them with water and got some goldfish from friends and dumped them into the tanks (no, not our friends).

In case someone from the Society for Prevention of Cruelty to Animals is reading this, we didn't actually dump them in; we placed them in the tanks with loving care.

A few survived the first winter. We replaced the unfortunate ones that were unable to adapt to being frozen solid through part of January and most of February.

Meanwhile, in the fall, the leaves fell from the trees and seemed to be attracted to the tanks. The decaying vegetation sapped the oxygen from the water and killed the survivors of the frozen tanks.

Goldfish have been around for at least a thousand years (the ones that weren't frozen). They're descended from a silver-colored member of the carp family that occasionally produced a mutated orange/red fish. The Chinese selectively bred these fish and they eventually became the goldfish we know today.

Our neighbor Rod has koi in his pond and they look like goldfish but they cost a lot more. They're the aristocrats of the carp family. The crafty Japanese apparently invented these fish for American tourists.

Great Blue Herons, the birds that happily eat fish you keep outside (or inside if they could open doors) don't really care how much you paid for your fish. Their moto is, "put 'em in in the tank and we eat 'em."

If what I have written inspires you to own goldfish, I recommend buying them from a pet shop. They're sometimes cheaper than the ones the bait shops sell. And if you want to keep them a while, thaw them out some time in late March.

Put them in water, and if they swim, you did it right.

YOU DON'T NEED A ROAD TO DRIVE IN THE FLINT HILLS

I'M NOT ABOVE criticizing younger people for texting while driving. I am concerned for their safety of course, but I'm a little worried about mine, too. If a texter (I suppose that's what you call them) swerves into my car at 60 mph or greater, I'll be just as dead as the texter.

When I was that age I didn't text anyone while I was driving. In fact, I didn't text at all because there wasn't anything to text on.

The roads were bad enough where I grew up that just keeping the car somewhere between the two ditches was a full-time job.

Out there in the Kansas oil fields, we not only didn't have smart phones, we didn't even have dumb phones. But it didn't matter because we wouldn't have had anything to talk about if a telephone had somehow materialized.

The only communication I recall was when my Dad met someone on the road in his lease car. They would park side-by-side and chat about a tank battery that was running over and destroying a farmer's corn crop. Or maybe they would just wave with the index finger that happened to be on the steering wheel and keep moving—35 mph or so.

I learned to drive in those days. I was about 10 years old and we had a 38 Chevy two-door sedan.

My Dad took me into the nearest pasture, making sure the spring cattle hadn't been let in yet (he didn't want me to run into a cow). He put the Chevy into low gear and told me to let the clutch out—slowly. I let it out, but not so slowly. We jumped, jerked and lurched, and finally got going in a kind of northeasterly direction.

If I had had a smart phone, I could have texted to my heart's content. I could also have taken my hands off the steering wheel while I was doing it. There was nothing to hit and even if there had been, I would have missed it—especially if I had been aiming for it.

"Follow the road," my Dad shouted.

"What road?" I asked.

The "road" was two paths made by the rancher's pickup wheels. In the Flint Hills, you can just drive out into the prairie anywhere you please without the danger of getting stuck because there isn't much dirt.

I tried my best to stay on the "road".But handling the steering wheel and the brake simultaneously was about all I could handle.

Using the brake is a bit of an exaggeration because when a 38 Chevy is in low gear you aren't going to stop it with a mere brake. It was geared pretty much like a tractor.

Later we got a 1940 Ford V/8 and I couldn't wait for Saturday night because I was allowed to drive when we got out of the lease roads and onto the main road. I drove until we were about a mile from town, then gave the wheel back to my Dad. He didn't want me driving in Madison traffic. It was a town of about 1,500 and on Saturday night you might get as many as three cars on Main Street at the same time.

About the time we got the Ford we moved into an oil field "camp" about nine miles from town and we got our first telephone. It was in an oak box hanging on the wall. On the right side was a crank that you used to "ring someone up." The speaker jutted out from the middle of the box and a receiver was kept in a hanger on the left side.

It was a party line with nine families on it. Each family had a "ring" such as a long and a short or two shorts and a long, etc. If you got a call from someone off the party line, an operator handled it.

But you could call someone on your own party line just by turning a couple of turns for a long and a quarter turn for a short. The person called would answer and the other seven people on the line could listen to your conversation. They were very quiet, but a sneeze would give them away.

My grandmother—when she didn't have much to do (much of the time)—sometimes would add a short or two to a call which resulted a good deal of confusion.

I'm sure that was more fun than texting and running into other cars.

CATARACT SURGERY
HELPS TO FIND YOUR GLASSES

I WAS 10 WHEN I got my first pair of glasses. This would have been in about 1938. They were gold rimmed and the lenses perfect circles. They were "geek" glasses, the kind Harry Potter wears.

I wore them because all spectacles were in the geek style then. I have astigmatism which makes some black lines kind of gray. I have eye balls more like footballs than basketballs.

At the time, we lived in the eastern Kansas oil fields and the closest town big enough for an eye doctor was Emporia, home town of the famous editor William Allen White. So we went there to a Dr. Tremble. I remember his name because it was written in gold on the hard metal glasses case.

I was apprehensive when he put drops in my eyes then left the room. I wondered if he would ever come back and whether I wanted him to.

My parents took me to a restaurant after the examination. I ordered chicken and corn on the cob. The meal came with small, round boiled potatoes. I could barely see the chicken let alone the potatoes.

Feeling around with my fork, I decided to divide the potatoes in half to make them more stable. I applied the fork to a heavily buttered potato and catapulted it onto the table next to us.

I had no idea what damage I had done to our neighboring diners because I couldn't see them. The waiter brought me another potato. I assume he removed the one that landed on the neighboring table. I stabbed at the fresh potato with the fork and cut it with my knife. I learned not to eat buttered potatoes when your eyes are dilated.

I had to come back a week or so later to get my glasses. The lenses were real glass and about as heavy as binoculars.

I wore them most of the time until I became a teenager. Geek glasses had begun to cramp my style so I got some rimless ones, the rage in the 1940s. But after a while they were geeky, too. So I got by without glasses. When I needed to see something, I squinted, which molded my eye balls into a more symmetrical shape temporarily.

That still isn't the end of it. I now have undergone cataract surgery and I can still see. In fact, I can see a little better than I did.

I also have glaucoma so I have to put medicine drops in my eyes two times a day.

As an old person, I am happy to mess with glasses and drops because I can see well enough to know what I am having for lunch.

There was a time when I resisted wearing glasses. Then I resisted wearing bifocals, then trifocals. But I was young and could see pretty well without glasses. At least I thought I could. My eye doctor thought otherwise and told me so every time I visited his office.

"You just wear your glasses when you have to see, don't you?" he often said, sarcasm oozing from his voice.

I said nothing, but I was thinking, "Duh!"

Eventually, I realized that vanity is second to vision. If you don't wear your glasses, how can you make fun of people who do?

A daughter wears contact lenses and she tells me they now make ones that correct astigmatism. I don't plan to try them.

My son wears dollar glasses he buys from the department store. I'm not sure they do the job, but it doesn't matter because he usually can't find them anyway.

CANOE TRIPS ARE FOR PEOPLE WHO SHOULD KNOW BETTER

BEFORE SHE RETIRED, my wife Dorothy worked in human resources at a regional medical center. Her coworkers became our friends and we did a lot of things together though, they were younger than we were.

One of those things was a canoe trip—over a Fourth of July weekend. This was not a simple jaunt across a farm pond. It was down the Illinois River in Oklahoma. I should have been happy that it was DOWN the river. We had enough problems without paddling against the current.

The Illinois is a 145-mile-long tributary of the Arkansas River and it is in parts of Arkansas and Oklahoma. The Osage Indians called it Ne-eng-wah-kon-dah, which means Medicine Stone River. I have other names for it.

Nobody told me how far we were paddling. I imagined it would be four or five miles. It turned out to be 50 miles.

Nobody told me the river was at flood stage. People were out with chain saws trying to clear the channels.

The fellow at the tour office said, "Don't worry, you can walk out of the river anywhere." He failed to mention I'd be walking under water.

To start our journey, we had to be transported several miles up river along with our canoes. We were riding on the back of a flat-bed truck and the boats were on a four-wheel trailer. I should have jumped off when I smelled burning rubber. A tire on the trailer blew out and the driver just kept going. We still had three good tires, didn't we?

We unloaded in a rocky area where just a little bit of water was running down river. The driver warned us of some people upstream. "Don't worry too much about them," he said. "They may act a little strange but they're probably not going to hurt you, but be careful at the big bridge. There's some pretty rowdy people over there. You don't want to mess with them."

I KNEW the "strange" people weren't going to hurt me because soon we were going to be far down stream. If they were going to be nasty, they would have to be swift paddlers. They were laughing and jumping up and down and appeared to be throwing something our way.

They were throwing firecrackers.

We wasted no time getting our boats into the river. Unfortunately, considering the fun the people were planning for us upstream, we probably could have spent a little more time tying our supplies in the vessels.

By "supplies" I mean our food (in plastic sacks) and a tent for each boat. This was to be an overnighter. Nobody told me that.

So the journey began. I was in the back so that I could counter Dorothy's moves with the paddle.

When we were headed toward a submerged tree trunk she frantically paddled on the side away from the hazard which had the effect of aiming the canoe at sure disaster. I back paddled in an attempt to miss the submerged object. Sometimes it worked. That is until the swift current brought the side of our canoe against a very large tree in the water.

I knew enough about canoeing to see that pushing off of the tree with a paddle over the side would not work. So I yelled, "Don't push off!" This occurred at the same time Dorothy was pushing off.

Water came in over the side—lots of water. We, along with our supplies were dunked into the river. I went down, down, down to where I could have walked out if I had enough time before I drowned. I swam upward. Soon I seemed to be breathing air, but I couldn't see anything. I had come up under the canoe.

No one told me our canoe might capsize and that I might surface beneath it, pretty scary when you aren't sure whether you are dead or alive.

I lost my cap and glasses, and we had barely gone far enough to avoid the firecrackers. The handles of our paddles fortunately were hollow. Unfortunately, the current sent them into some tree roots in swift water. I did not want to swim over to get them so one of the younger members of the party got them for us

We paddled and paddled and the sun was going down. I suggested we start looking for a place to camp. We could make it a little farther, I was told by our friends who were dry.

After what seemed like hours of whining, the others decided to humor me and put up the tents–in the dark. We propped our bedding around the fire, which didn't do much to dry it out, but made spectacular smoke.

I sat in our canoe which rolled on its keel as I sliced a tough steak on a flimsy paper plate. We got our tent up though my side was on a tree limb. It didn't matter because I couldn't sleep in wet clothes anyway. We got up at sunrise and found that we had pitched our tent in the middle of stinging nettles. The next thing we noticed was that we had made camp under the bridge we were supposed to avoid.

The rest of the trip down still water was uneventful except for the ticks.

I'll do more independent research before I take another canoe trip.

OUR CAT ISN'T SUPER SMART
JUST SMARTER THAN WE ARE

YOU KNOW YOU'RE becoming a doddering, old coot when you start writing about your cat. For me, it's worse because I'm writing about my wife's cat. Why? That is a question to which I do not know the answer (notice the fancy grammar—another sign of creeping senility).

When our kids were still living at home, I seldom told anyone they were smarter than other neighborhood children. That's because for the most part, they weren't. And if they were, the neighbors wouldn't believe it because they knew their kids were a lot smarter.

Cats are different. I will say without hesitation that our car is smarter than any of the other cats in our neighborhood (we live in the country and there aren't any cats within a mile or so).

You can ask why my wife chose to name the cat Sarah, but I would be unable to give you a sensible answer. Her thinking probably was that the most unlikely name for a cat is Sarah, therefor her name is Sarah.

Sarah is a calico, which I thought was a cat with a questionable family history, a cat with a few skeletons in her closet. That is not exactly true.

Now comes the educational part of the column:

Calicos are mostly white, with patches of two other colors, usually orange and black. If these two colors have tabby patterns, the cat is called a Caliby. That's what ours is. In Quebec (where they speak French) the cats are sometimes called chatte d'Espagne which means "cat from Spain." This is laughable because lots of cats come from Spain, and most of them are not calicos. They are simply Spanish cats.

Besides, it seems to me that if you're going to call a calico cat a chatte d'Espagne, you ought to do it in Spanish, not French.

Calico is not a breed, just a color pattern.

It may be discriminatory, but calico cats are nearly always female. That's because the genetic determination of some coat colors in cats is linked to the X chromosome. And, because of these genetics, calico males usually have impaired vitality (to put it delicately) and are almost always sterile.

There is no shame in this..

She does not meow and she doesn't purr. She doesn't like to sit on your lap (not all bad) and she doesn't like company.

71

She sleeps all day and roams at night.

She won't eat her cat food unless the bowl is heaping full. If she can see the bottom of the container and you don't fill it, she'll go outside and catch a mouse. Like most cats, she brings the dead mouse to our doorstep. If the door were open, she would no doubt bring her prize inside. I've heard it said that cats do this to show their love. They are presenting you something that is dear to them.

I think cats drag a dead mouse or rat to your door to show contempt. They're telling you in a graphic way that "you didn't fill my bowl to the top, so here's a dead mouse. How do you like THAT?"

When Sarah wants to go out at night and we're asleep, she walks across our bodies—and she's heavy. She climbs up the roof to get to a small deck near our bed and sits on a railing. When she wants in, she jumps to the floor of the deck, making a thumping sound. If we don't let her in, she thumps again, and again, and again.

When not a lot is going on outside at night, she gets bored and wants in. Later she gets even more bored and begins her walks across our supine bodies. This continues through the night.

At daybreak she wisely hides so that we can't wake her up and throw her outside. She has many hiding places and won't budge when called.

She's not all that smart, just smarter than we are.

IT WAS AN UGLY BIRD
AND IT SEEMED TO LIKE US

IT WAS ABOUT 10 a.m. in late fall and my son had come over for breakfast. We were gazing toward the road which borders our 20 acres on the east.

"Hey, Tedd," I said, "look at the big turkey coming up the hill."

"I don't think that's a turkey," he said, "It's way too big."

As it came closer, I could see that he was right. This was a really big bird. It looked like an ostrich. But we don't see many ostriches in Kansas. Fact is, we don't see any ostriches.

It was an emu. At the time, people had been buying emu pairs to breed. The goal was to get rich. The only people getting rich were the people selling the emus. Prospective emu ranchers were told that the meat was like steak, and the oil could be sold for a lot of money.

No one told them how to get the emus to give them the oil or where to sell it if they got some. And, as we later discovered, emu meat may look like steak but doesn't taste much like it.

We had six cows at the time. We decided to put the emu in the west pasture and send my wife out to find out which emu farm was missing a bird. None of the "ranchers" would admit that they knew what an emu was. And they certainly didn't want one.

So Tedd and I started shooing the bird toward the open gate. There was a big tree against the fence near the gate, and the emu would reach the tree, turn around and go back the way he came. We tried several times with the same result. We finally got an extension ladder which the emu followed. As it got to the end of the ladder we turned it toward the gate. The bird went in and we closed the gate.

We were stuck with a bird nearly seven feet tall, with legs strong enough to kill you and a brain the size of a human eyeball.

When winter came we had to feed it. They eat grasshoppers and grass, neither of which is plentiful in Kansas in the winter. I had to buy feed. Emu feed isn't plentiful in Kansas either, so I settled for chicken feed—lots of chicken feed.

I moved the cows into the pasture with the bird, and no one was happy.

Cows and emus don't mix. An emu can reach 6 feet 3 inches in height and can run about 30 miles an hour for extended periods.

73

They weigh about 88 pounds—dry.

That doesn't sound so heavy, but when it's hungry and running toward you and you have a bucket of chicken feed, 88 pounds is like 888. An emu is not a cute, little wren. It's a big, ugly bird with feet made for running—and whacking anyone who doesn't let of the feed fast enough.

The emu has a beak made for pecking a large hole in your head.

Every time the bird came to get its feed, the cows would chase it away. Ordinarily that was fine with me, but that meant I had to run after the bird to get it fed. I put out a bale of hay then ran with the chicken feed before the cows finished the hay.

I decided it would be wise to feed the cows in another place, so I put the feeding trough in the corral that had a gate opening into the pasture where the emu was. I kept the gate shut. I was a novice rancher but not as dumb as the cows thought I was.

The cows were black with white faces. Hazel, was mostly Holstein and much larger than the others. She was the leader of the herd—and you had better believe it, especially if you were a big, ugly bird.

One day the gate was left open (big mistake) and the emu wandered into the corral. If I could have spoken emu, I would have advised against this. The cows weren't happy. Hazel was downright disgusted.

She pawed the ground, put her head down and shook it side to side, snorted and generally looked unfriendly. The emu didn't appear to be afraid (another big mistake).

Hazel charged and the feathers flew. The emu tried to find the opening in the fence but apparently forgot where it was. He repeatedly hit the fence and Hazel sent the non-flying bird flying. Eventually she butted it through the opening, and it departed, appearing to exceed its 30 mph top speed.

The emu, apparently embarrassed, took it out on a hapless coyote that chanced to lope into the pasture. If I could have spoken coyote, I would have advised him not to do that. The emu chased the coyote across the pasture, nipping at its rear all the way. The coyote was able to scoot under the fence and save itself.

With the cows in one pasture and the emu in another, I left the gate open where the emu was, hoping it would run away. No such luck. It apparently liked us.

SHOWER CONTROLS IMPRESS BUT I'M AFRAID TO USE THEM

WE'VE BEEN LIVING with a fiberglass shower the past 26 years or so, and what's worse, it's BROWN. Why would anyone put a brown shower in a house? We didn't. It was there when we bought the house.

I'm sure you're wondering why the original owner of the house would install a brown, fiberglass shower. The answer is because it matched the brown toilet and bathtub. Colored bathroom appliances were the rage in 1980 when the house was built.

You probably won't believe this but one of the down-stairs bathrooms had a pink sink and toilet. PINK! Naturally, we replaced them with a blander color when we remodeled that bathroom.

A little more than a month ago I decided I couldn't take one more bath in a brown, fiberglass shower.

We hired a friend who had installed some windows in our dining room to build us a new shower and to increase the height of the vanity for a more modern look. We decided to keep the brown tub. No one would actually see us using it anyway.

It took a little more than a month to tear out the old shower and build a new and larger one with tiled walls and a glass partition and door. It has a stylish shower head that sprays a lot of water and a second head on a flexible chromed hose (snazzy).

The controls are similar to those on a Boeing 747. Happily, the shower does not fly (as far as I know).

These controls are impressive but daunting.

Dorothy and I had been taking our showers down stairs in what we call the gray room. We call it that because the tub and sink are gray as are the walls and the floor tile. But that's okay because gray is in again.

The shower in that room is part of the bathtub setup and it's gray fiberglass. But it looks modern (sort of). Like many of these setups, the tub is slippery, especially for old folks like us. So we put one of those plastic mats in it. It has suction cups on the bottom and on the top are plastic nodules that dig into your feet.

Dorothy thinks it's stimulating, but I think it's like standing on rocks.

Actually, the pebbles were more inviting than trying to figure out how to get water that didn't burn or freeze you in the new shower.

Meanwhile, you are standing unclothed and at the mercy of modern technology. The water faucet (if you can call it that) has two levers, one for water and one for temperature.

You stand there a prisoner enclosed in glass hoping you turn the right one and that it's in the right direction.

Eventually I decided I had to bite the bullet so to speak and actually take a shower in it. I turned the big handle assuming it was water. I was right. Cold, shiver-inducing water streamed out in a blast and splashed against my unprotected chest.

I'm thinking, "I've got to get this turned off NOW or I will die of exposure." But I was afraid to move. What if I turned it the wrong way and it got colder? Then I saw the smaller, lever. Maybe it was heat. I turned it and blessed warmth ensued. I would LIVE.

I turned it up until it was scalding hot. Better to be cooked than frozen, I thought. Maybe not.

Once I got the water regulated to some semblance of comfort, it wasn't half bad. So I stayed in the new shower until my skin was beginning to look like a blood hound's neck.

I turned off the water and grabbed for a towel. I had left it outside the shower. I had also forgotten to put the bath mat down. So I stepped out wet into the cold bathroom, slipping a bit on the tile.

I quickly dried off and looked back in the shower and spotted a shower head on a flexible hose. It had three buttons on it for adjusting heat and spray. I'm not touching that thing.

IF HOLES ARE SHALLOW THEY SEEM MUCH STRAIGHTER

THIS IS ABOUT notable holes I have dug. You're thinking, "Uh-oh, he's finally flipped." My first occurred when I was about 7.

I found my Dad's shovel and thought, "why not dig a hole?" I didn't stop until the surface was waist high. (not very deep).

Dad was not pleased. He filled in the hole and hung the shovel higher.

The hole later came in handy. It filled with water and the loose dirt sank, leaving a depression, mostly mud.

My dog Jack was part terrier and hated snakes. One day a rattler bit him and he got sick (the dog). To ease the pain, he soaked his face in the mud hole (the only medical procedure he was familiar with at the time). He got well and apparently developed an immunity to the bites. He would be sick for a few days then shake it off and look for more snakes.

I dug a lot of holes after that, but only a few notable ones. I discovered that the hydrants at our place near Rose Hill, south of Wichita, didn't work. The pipes were corroded so I decided to replace them. That meant digging a long, narrow hole, often called a ditch.

I remembered that using a shovel is a lot of work. The ditch would extend from the well to the old feed barn, then to the north side of the house then to the east end, quite a distance.

I rented a motorized ditch digger. After he had my money, the rental guy was probably thinking, "I'd refund his money if I could see the ditch he's going to dig."

The digger had handles. You hung onto them and walked backward as the machine dug four feet into the ground. You saw where you'd been but not where you were going. It turned out that I wasn't going very far.

The rental guy said the machine had a "dead man's switch." I didn't like the sound of that, but he explained that it shut itself off if something strange happened.

Something strange happened. I passed the big elm tree. The engine made a mighty roar, and I found myself gazing at the clouds.

I had run the machine into a root tough enough to toss the machine out of the ditch and me on my back in the dirt.

Later, my son Tedd and I were building a fence. Dorothy and I had six cows at the time, and we thought a fence would be handy.

So We rented a motorized posthole digger that also had handlebars. We turned it on (big mistake) and each grabbed a handlebar. That was to keep the hole perpendicular to the surface. Instead, it whirled Tedd and me in a circle and dug itself several holes in random places. We were doing slant-hole drilling before the oil companies discovered it.

We had notable holes though they weren't exactly where we wanted them. We learned that if you want holes perpendicular to the surface, you should dig only really shallow ones.

LOOK IN THE SPIDER'S EYES TO GET TO KNOW HIM BETTER

THIS IS A "HUMOR" column, so I thought I'd write about spiders. If I were a bug, I'd be laughing because spiders have an extra pair of legs. They belong to a phylum called arachnid.

In Greek, that means "spider." Well, Duh! Spiders can't fly because they don't have wings. They don't have antennae either, so they have nothing to wiggle. But they can be scary because some of them have venom that can hurt you.

We have an untidy spider in our house. He or she (we want to be politically correct—spiders have feelings) lives in the base board. We never see it, but we know it's there because we see its leftovers.

This spider probably is laughing all eight of its socks off when it scatters insect parts on the floor. We sweep them away and they soon reappear. Has he no shame?

I know a thing or two about spiders because I had time to observe them when I was a little boy. We had an outhouse that spiders loved. I can't tell you why. I certainly didn't love it. But, then I obviously am not a spider (I have only two legs).

It would have been impossible to kill all of them so my plan was wary acceptance. I didn't bother them and I hoped they wouldn't bother me. I had the same deal with the wasps.

I may be prejudiced, but I just don't like most spiders, particularly the brown recluse ones. Some people say they have a violin mark on them. Unfortunately, so do a lot of other spiders.

You have to look into the brown recluse's eyes to identify them. Most spiders have eight eyes, but brown recluse spiders have only six. I'm not about to look into the eyes of a brown recluse spider. I'll just take his word for it.

If you're getting weary of this "him or her" stuff, why not just find out the sex of the spider? The problem is that it's difficult to determine the sex of a spider. Sometimes you have to look through a microscope. I doubt that the average spider would hold still long enough for that, and besides, even a spider is entitled to some privacy.

When we lived in Coffeyville we had big, hairy tarantulas. Driving at night you could see their eyes reflected in the headlights.

People said they were harmless, and I suppose they were, but I didn't want them in bed with me.

One day the preacher and his family came to dinner at our house and slinking out of a planter in the floor of the living room was a large tarantula. I grabbed a two by four and took a swing at it. I missed the spider, and happily, the minister, too. The spider retreated into the plants never to be seen again.

And that was just fine with me.

WHEAT GOES TO THE BELLY AND MAKES IT FATTER

I READ A BOOK a while back by a physician who wrote in 50,000 words or so that we shouldn't eat wheat. His premise was that wheat the hunters and gatherers ate was okay, but modern wheat has been modified so much that it isn't good for us.

The hunters and gatherers probably didn't get any ill effects from wheat because they didn't get enough of it. By the time they had hunted some the birds had already gathered most of it.

A lot of technical jargon in the book explains that wheat goes right to the belly and makes it a lot bigger. I've got news for the doctor. Wheat is not the only thing that does that.

The government tells us to eat all the wheat we can because it has fiber and tastes better than rope. Wheat is big in the food pyramid.

I tried to eliminate wheat from my diet to alleviate my allergies. Have you ever tried to do that? Nearly everything in the grocery store except the customer assistance department has wheat in it. Some of the stuff—cereals, for example—are pretty much all wheat, except for some chemicals.

Wheat is an important part of nearly all bread, even rye bread. All kinds of breads have some wheat in them to make them stick together. The part that makes bread stick together is gluten (think glue). And that's not good for a lot of people either.

For something that may be bad for you, a lot of research has gone into making bread fit what the government says you need—high-fiber grain.

The bread makers decided that if the wheat is good in bread, why not add other grains like barley and flax and anything else the birds leave behind. I looked on the wrapper of the bread in our kitchen and it has seven grains in it.

In the 1930s and 40s we lived in the country and got to town once a week. We were on a Star route which had contract mail carriers. They drove their own cars and were allowed to bring stuff to you from town.

We got a loaf of Playboy Bread in the mail twice a week. It was so refined you could squeeze it into a little gray mass the size of a golf ball. I'm probably still digesting some of that Playboy Bread.

Bread has changed. It used to be super white and small enough to get lost in the toaster. But the loaf was longer and you got more slices.

Now the seven-grain bread is tall but there are fewer slices, none of which will fit in the toaster.

You have to put it in on its side then turn it over when it pops up. That's if you can get it out of the wrapper. It's plastic on the outside with a tie to keep it closed. Inside, is a different kind of plastic that is ironed shut. Try to get it undone and you will either tear it apart or resort to the scissors.

I cut down on bread by making a sandwich with only one piece of bread. This reduces the calories but kind of defeats the purpose of a sandwich. That is to have something to hold the meat with. The Earl of Sandwich knew what he was doing.

Using just one slice cuts the calories but the meat and lettuce and tomato keep falling off.

There was a time when I made bread. I even got a grinder so that I could make my own flour, and I learned a lot. I learned that you should not start bread late in the evening. I did that once and I was up most of the night pushing the risen bread down, a necessary part of the process.

So if you have a problem with someone in your family, and revenge is your aim, mix a batch of bread at about 10 p.m. and leave town.

My grandmother made wonderful bread with yeast from a starter she kept on a shelf on her wood cooking stove. It was a pinch of the dough from her last batch of bread. The loaves were tall and crusty and tasted great with a glass of fresh buttermilk.

The slices were too tall and wide to fit in a toaster. But that didn't matter because she didn't have a toaster.

I DON'T REALLY GIVE A HOOT
WHAT AN OWL HAD FOR BREAKFAST

WE HAVE OWLS at our place. I hear them from time to time, and they really do sound like they're saying "who." I know they're not actually saying anything unless it's some kind of owl-to-owl communication.

That doesn't make a lot of sense because it's kind of repetitive. I'm sure it would get tiresome to ask a question over and over and never get an answer, assuming you wanted to know what a bird had to say.

Apparently more than one kind of owl says "who" and that's not the only thing they say. They also whistle and growl. I assume they whistle when they're happy and growl when they're upset—like when a hawk gets a mouse they had their eye on.

When I was teaching at Friends University the biology professor heard that we had owls on our place. He wanted me to watch for owl barf. I said, "You've got to be kidding."

He said it could indicate what the owl ate. I'm thinking, "Who cares?"

You may not believe this—I didn't—but the ornithologists have a name for it. It's a pellet, the undigested parts of a bird's food.

These pellets can tell ornithologists something about the bird's diet. They look for the exoskeletons of bugs, indigestible plant matter, bones, fur, feathers, bills, claws and teeth. In falconry the pellet is called a casting. Calling it that doesn't make it any less disgusting. Pellets are collected to analyze the seasonal variation in a bird's eating habits.

Having been a non-ornithologist all of my life, I don't care a lot about the seasonal variation of an owl's eating habits. I don't even care what an owl had for breakfast this morning. If an owl wants to eat a mouse or two or a grasshopper, I say that's his (or her) business.

I didn't know this until recently but wild turkeys are omnivores, too. For you non-scientific readers, an omnivore eats plants and other animals. I thought turkeys ate just plants, like seeds and grass and stuff.

They're actually non discriminating diners. They eat insects, grains, spiders, snails, slugs, salamanders, small lizards, small frogs, millipedes, grasshoppers, VERY small snakes, worms, grasses, vines, flowers, acorns, buds and seeds among other things.

Turkeys are not the brightest birds, but why would they eat salamanders?

Why would anything eat a slug? Salamanders are amphibians like frogs, and lucky for turkeys, salamanders can regenerate lost limbs and body parts. They have no more than four fingers on the front legs and no more than five on the rear legs.

But back to the owls. I'm sure we have others, but the ones we see from time to time are great horned owls. They don't really have horns, but the feathers on their heads look like horns or the ears of a cat. It would have been confusing to call them great ears of a cat owls.

They aren't particular what they catch and eat. They grab raccoons, rabbits, squirrels, domestic birds like chickens, falcons, cats and dogs occasionally and other owls. They regularly eat skunks.

Once in a while a great horned owl will attack humans if they get too close to the nest. A great horned owl can be up to two feet long, have a five-foot wing span and weigh nearly six pounds.

So if you're a human or a skunk, it's best to avoid the owl's nest.

THE MALE LIP IS IMPORTANT AS A PLACE TO GROW WHISKERS

A FEW MONTHS AGO I wrote a very important column about men who wish they were younger, men who let their whiskers grow into a five o'clock shadow effect that presumably is "irresistible" to women.

My research shows that this irresistibility is more often mentioned by men with whiskers than by women.

Nothing much has happened with this subject since I wrote the last time, but I have to apologize for not including the male lip in my earlier coverage. The lip, of course, has been a whisker factor for many years. I refer to the mustache. Some of the same men who favor the five o'clock-shadow look are also partial to hair on the lip.

The mustache has been around for a long time. In the 14th Century when King James came to the British throne he had a dapper mustache. His son King Charles I, made the handlebar variety popular. Every man of fashion copied it.

Unfortunately for the King, Oliver Cromwell, who had a much smaller mustache, had the King executed. History does not record whether it was because of the mustache.

As you have no doubt noticed, there are many kinds of mustaches. There is even more than one way of spelling them, and no doubt some reader will let me know that I have spelled it incorrectly.

Well, before you do that, here's the difference. Moustache is the British spelling, and mustache is the preferred American way. So to make things clear, I'll use each in a sentence along with a bonus Spanish spelling.

BRITISH: The prime minister had crumpet crumbs in his moustache. AMERICAN: The cowboy rode happily into the sunset until his mustache got caught in his spurs. Or, SPANISH: El vaquero twirled his mustachio and rode el caballo into the sunset while eating a jalapeno.

I hope we weren't too technical. Though we strive to be entertaining, we can't pass up a chance to educate. We feel it's our duty to our readers.

But back to the different kinds. There's the handlebar mentioned earlier. It's shaped like the handlebars on a Harley, the ones that a 6-foot biker has to stand up in the saddle to reach.

The pencil mustache is carefully trimmed and goes well with a Panama hat. It's often worn by Bolivian drug dealers. Notable wearers in the past were Duke Ellington and Robert Benchley. Movie pirates wore them, too.

Then there's the Fuller brush mustache. It's the bushy type that covers the entire upper lip with hair about two inches thick. If there is white foam in it, your beer has a good head on it.

I had that kind of mustache for a while when I was in high school. I drove a dairy truck delivering milk, cream, butter and ice cream, and the guy who taught me the route had a Fuller mustache which I envied. So I grew one. No one noticed it, and I shaved it off.

So the mustache is not just an example of male vanity. There are some possible benefits:

1. It takes less time to shave—that is if you're into shaving at all. The space below the nose takes up about a third of the face and the lip takes a third of that space, so you could save as much as 30 to 45 seconds depending on your attachment to neatness.

2. Your lip stays warmer, eliminating the need for a ski mask with no opening for the mouth.

3. If you are a trumpet player, a mustache keeps your lip stiffer for the high notes.

So if people make sport of your mustache, tell them your doctor prescribed it for a cold lip.

TOOLS TO MAKE THINGS EASY CAN MAKE THINGS HARDER

I HAVE HAD A LONG association with the typewriter. It began when I was about 8 years old. I got a toy one for Christmas. It had a metal disk with upper and lower-case letters and numbers, zero through nine.

There were two metal keys. You pushed one to make the disk hit the ribbon and leave a letter or number on the paper. You banged the other key to bring the disk back for another letter.

You had to strike the two keys with your fist to get a good impression. I wrote a lot of short letters.

Then when I was a sophomore in high school my Dad thought it would be wise to take typing. I resisted, of course. Then I got to thinking. My Dad was right.

I was the only male in a class of 30 girls. I should have listened to him more often.

As it turned out, I became a journalist and typing came in handy.

When I joined the Air Force in 1950 I went through basic training with entertainers and musicians. I was to serve in a military band, but someone who looked at my records learned that I could type. So I spent the next four years typing military forms and requisitions.

Most of the newspapers I worked for later used Royal typewriters. I had an old Underwood at home and later a Royal portable. For much of my life I had gloried in the clacking noise the typewriter made. It set up a rhythm that made typing easier.

Then along came the digital age.

I was working at the Wichita Eagle when it went partially digital. This was in the late 1970s.

The system worked with IBM Selectric typewriters. They were electrified and if you pressed a key and didn't immediately remove your finger, the letter would keep typing. I have a slow "L" finger so when I typed "level" it came out lllllevelllll.

We had special paper that had several carbons and the typewriter ribbons were different. They were a deep black so that the copy could be scanned and set into type using a digital system the size of a three-car garage.

We had symbols to change the type face and size of the type. If we made a mistake, we had a pen to remove the offending word or words.

I volunteered to get the first Selectric and blundered into the digital world. Because of the large number of "Ls" I typed, my typing was much slower using the tools that were designed to speed things up.

We used symbols to tell the computer what to do. The paper's body type, for example, was 8 point, and an asterisk was its symbol. I was the Eagle's oil editor and I also edited a weekly business page.

New oil and gas wells were set into agate type, barely legible without a magnifying glass. There was a lot of this type on the business page.

Soon after the paper went digital, I sent the new wells list to the composing room.

Unfortunately, I had neglected to type the symbol for agate type. Earlier I had sent some headlines in 36-point (about a half inch high in some type faces). I forgot to change the symbol and the agate type was set in 36 point.

The composing room sent the proof up to me in a huge roll. I stood on a desk and tossed it out to see how long it was. It went all the way across the newsroom.

If there are people around who worked there then, they probably are still laughing. I say to them: "Shut up."

THERE MAY BE NO CURE FOR A NOUN DISEASE

I DON'T REMEMBER the name of the book but it was about how to remember things. I'm trying to recall the book because I'm having a problem with names. I don't have anything against names; I just can't remember them.

I have a noun disease.

As I recall, and I don't, really, the book described a method for remembering. It used association. You think up a ridiculous story that represents the thing you are trying to remember.

This should be a piece of cake. Any story I think up is going to be ridiculous.

Let's say I'm trying to remember the actor Michael Caine. He is in a movie that I want to recommend to a friend. Caine is not getting any younger so I create a mental picture of an old person walking with a CANE. You have to imagine this person doing something, so you have him trying to get onto a train (rhymes with Caine) and he can't make it up the first step and he falls down.

So later I think to myself, who is the guy in the movie I want to recommend? The old man with the cane pops into my mind, but unfortunately I can't imagine why. I'm thinking the movie must be Citizen Kane. Unfortunately, that movie isn't showing. No, it's a person named Caine. Boris Caine? Nancy Cane? Candy Cain? Wait! It's Michael Caine, the movie star.

But what's the movie? I haven't the foggiest idea. I forgot to include it in the mental picture.

Another trick is called "meet and repeat." If you hear a person's name, for example, don't just nod and continue talking. Plug the name into what you're saying.

For example, "and so, George Alton Korsinski, as I was saying, Mr. Lorsinki, or actually, what I meant to say, Mr. George, I have lost my train of thought . . ."

When your spouse asks, "Who was that guy you were talking to?" You can say with confidence, "Lars Cazooski," "I think he's related to Michael Caine. Incidentally, I hear he fell down and broke his arm the other day."

Collectively, our memories are getting fuzzier.

A recent poll found that people between 18 and 34 are more likely than us older folks to forget what day it is and where they put their keys.

In their defense, we older folks don't forget what day it is, we just don't care. And, we don't forget our keys because what good are they if we can't find our car?

Years ago I read about the Cicero method of remembering. Of course, Cicero spoke in Latin and I don't remember much Latin.

Anyway, the idea is to go through the rooms in your house. I say YOUR house because the neighbors won't understand if you go through their house. As you walk through the rooms in your mind's eye, attach the things you are trying to memorize to each room.

Let's say you are trying to remember a list of unrelated words. Why? Because if you don't remember them correctly, who cares?

Consider a list of everyday objects: a knife, a pencil, a dog and a Mercedes. We stroll through the kitchen and see a paring knife, then we go through the hallway and there is a pencil sharpener on the wall. In the living room there's a poodle on the couch. We move out the front door and there's a Mercedes. The driver, trying to remember a movie starring Michael Caine, got distracted, jumped the curb and ended up on your front porch.

Every time you go through a room in your house you will recall another object that you don't want to remember. So, you'll have to go back through the house in your mind's eye and remove each object so you won't have to keep remembering it.

It can become downright tedious so let's just forget the whole thing.

A GOOD WAY TO CALM A HORSE IS TO FEED IT SOME GARLIC

I GREW UP in the Flint Hills around cowhands who were as familiar with their horses as people are today with their cars. But despite the association with horsemen, I am not one myself. In fact, my experiences with horses have been disappointing and now and then disastrous. Once a neighbor invited us to spend a weekend at his ranch near Cripple Creek, CO.

We knew we were on a ranch when in the middle of the night I flushed a toilet and the lights went out. Electricity was provided by a generator and the house water pump used the same power line as the rest of the ranch.

The next day we agreed to help move cattle to another pasture.

The ranch foreman saddled up what he referred to as a "gentle" horse for me. He adjusted the stirrups as short as they would go, which was about two inches below my Reeboks. I could not stand up in the saddle, a necessity if I didn't want a sore behind.

So I bounced around in the saddle all day long. My "gentle" horse was calm enough as long as the cattle were bunched together and progressing in the right direction. But when a cow wandered off, my horse took off after her without any urging from me.

The chase went on through brush, briar patches, clumps of cactus or low hanging limbs. And it didn't stop until the cow was back with the herd. If I was scraped off into something with stickers in it, that was my problem. No amount of pulling on the reins and shouting, "WHOA" or something more uncouth made any difference.

At the end of the day I couldn't sit down and didn't want to stand up.

More recently I had an equally disturbing experience with a horse I wasn't even sitting on. We were keeping a mare at our place for one of my wife Dorothy's friends. We have a horse barn and corral along with a place to store tack, but thankfully, no horses.

Our fences were designed for sheep, and horses don't pay much attention to them because they're taller than sheep. So we put a strand of barbed wire across the top of the fence, and that kept the horse where we could keep an eye on her.

She spent lots of time at the fence looking sadly on the other side.

One day a gate was inadvertently left open and the mare escaped. I was standing near the garden.

91

The horse came bounding out, headed straight for me. When a full-grown horse runs toward you at full speed and you are on the ground in front of it, that horse could just as well be a charging rhino. You want desperately to be somewhere else.

Lucky for me, the horse saw garlic growing in the garden, and to a horse recently freed from the slammer, that's as good as alfalfa. She ate garlic until not even a romantically-inclined horse would want to get near her. Then she kicked up her heels and went for the carrots.

I couldn't get her to do anything. We called her owner who brought a bucket of oats and a halter. The garlic fest was over

OIL FIELD SHOTGUN HOUSES WERE THE FIRST TINY HOUSES

IF YOU WATCH HGTV on cable, I'm sure you've seen the new trend in homes, the tiny house. It's like a mobile home, but smaller. It's on wheels so that it can be moved to a favorite spot.

These miniature abodes cost about six times the amount we paid for a two-bedroom house in the 1960s. I realize that was a long time ago, but the house did have a bathtub large enough to sit in.

Young people want to travel, attend costly entertainment events and otherwise amuse themselves and they can afford to do this only if they don't spend a lot of money on a place to live.

I apologize for being a spoilsport, but we had tiny homes in the oil fields in the 1930s and 1940s.

What's more, there was no loft and no miniature bathtub that most people don't fit in. We had no bathtub at all. This was because there wasn't room for one and there was no running water to put into it. We had no loft to sleep in because there was a cable running through the attic to keep the house from blowing away. It was attached to a 10-foot length of eight-inch pipe buried in the ground on each side of the house.

These oil field shacks were called shotgun houses. Those of us who lived in them assumed they were so named because a bullet fired through the front door went out the back door without hitting a wall.

Actually a shotgun house usually has one room leading into the other one without hallways. This style of house is well suited for hot climates because you can open the front and back doors and the breeze will flow through the entire house.

As I remember it, you didn't need this breeze because enough came through the cracks in the floor and around the windows that you didn't need to open the doors.

These little houses were set on a cement block at each corner. There was no foundation, so the Kansas wind could blow up under the house and through the cracks. Our house had linoleum on the floor of one room and it would lift off of the floor when the wind hit 30 miles an hour or so.

These shacks had a living room and a bedroom. A 9 x 12 rug fit to the walls. The kitchen was a lean-to on the bedroom.

It had a small cabinet bought in a furniture store and a cook stove.

There was no electricity, just natural gas that came from a nearby well. The rooms except for the kitchen had one gas light in the center of the ceiling. Heat was provided by a coal stove converted to gas.

The wood shingled roof leaked in several places and when it rained we waited until the water broke through the beaverboard ceiling then placed pots under the leaks. In a really hard rain we usually ran out of pots. This is not to say that our house was neglected—all of the oil field shacks were this way. The roofs had been repaired until the patches outnumbered the shingles.

If an oil company employee had to move, the house went with him. It was jacked up and placed on a wagon that was pulled by a six-horse team to the next location. There were "skinners" (teamsters) who made a living moving these houses with their magnificent draft horses.

We didn't feel deprived because everyone who worked in the oil fields then lived in these houses.

They were originally fairly well built but suffered a little every time they were moved, and over the years, most of them had been moved several times. The strain of jacking them up and and dropping them on a wagon and then moving them over rough gravel roads opened up cracks, some of them large enough to let in unwanted "visitors."

That included bugs and occasionally snakes. That's where hospitality usually ended.

I FEEL A LITTLE SILLY
TALKING TO A WHEEL

OUR FAMILY CAR is a four-door sedan with a lot of navigation equipment that is complicated for a person my age, though my great grandson no doubt could operate it even though he can't talk yet.

If he could talk, he probably would say, "What's the problem? You have a smart phone, don't you?"

Well, yes I do, but I don't understand it either.

According to the manual that came with the car, I'm supposed to synchronize the phone with the car's navigation system. Then I can make calls by just talking to the steering wheel. The problem is that I don't ever call anyone when I'm in the car, and if I did, I would feel silly talking to a steering wheel.

That's partly because I don't understand the system and partly because I don't really want to talk to anyone.

And if someone were to call me, I would be in a panic and might just jump out on the highway. So, I leave the smart phone at home.

The navigation system also has a GPS that tells me how to get places, often close to the place I want to go. That is if I knew how to type in the destination. First I have to know where to type it, and I haven't discovered that yet.

I thought I had it once, and I couldn't get the robot lady to talk to me. Later I inadvertently pushed a button that got her to talk and she kept sending me down roads I didn't know existed.

The system uses maps that have been downloaded to the car's computer. These maps aren't always up-to-date. The last time I used it, the robot lady sent me down a road that dead-ended at a four-year-old construction site (not anywhere near where I wanted to go).

I had to backtrack, and that forced the robot lady to re-compute, which really upset her. If you don't know where you're going, and worse, don't know exactly where you are, you don't want to make the robot lady angry.

The car is a hybrid, which means it has gasoline engine and an electric motor powered by a big battery.

The electric motor kicks in to save fuel. I was confused by this when we first acquired the car.

When I stopped for a red light there was total silence. I kept thinking the engine had died and I needed to restart it. It hadn't died, it just shut itself off (very eerie).

Starting the car is different, too. Turn the ignition key to "on" and you expect to hear the engine turn over. But you hear nothing. The needle on the speedometer goes all the way to the right past 100 mph and then back to zero. A little green light in the shape of a car comes on. That's it.

Put it in reverse, and the car silently backs out of the garage.

Sometimes I yearn for the days when the starter ground away, chipping teeth off of the flywheel, and the car coughed to a start, spewing blue smoke everywhere. Or, the starter clicked a few times and died. At least you knew it was alive before it died.

I haven't figured out the sound system either. The User's Guide says it's part of the navigation system.

I'm admittedly out of touch, but does that make sense?

IF FURNITURE IS IN THE WAY
I'M GOING TO WALK AROUND IT

A FEW WEEKS AGO I had a big, white bandage on my right arm that extended from my elbow to my wrist, and it caused people some discomfort, not to mention some discomfort for me.

Unless I wore a shirt that covered my knuckles, the bandage was noticeable. It was so noticeable, in fact, that people looked at their toes or a loose board in the floor to avoid mentioning it. It was like carrying a sign that said, "I've been injured; pity me."

People no doubt thought, "What happened to HIM?" A car wreck? An attack by carpenter ants? Said the wrong thing to some testy bikers?

I could have said I stumbled into a hornet's nest and got stung 322 times, but it didn't happen. I could have told them big bandages are a fashion statement, but everyone knows I'm not very fashionable.

The truth is the orchestra was rehearsing and I stumbled and fell over the director's podium. I can't hear you but I know you're laughing, and that's deplorable.

I was embarrassed. I knew people were thinking, "The old coot probably can't see and he thought it was someone's coat."

Our church choir presents special music at various times with musicians from Wichita State University and the Wichita Symphony. It was the day before the service, and the orchestra and choir were rehearsing separately.

The orchestra had completed its part and the choir was ready to practice before bringing both groups together. The choir arrived early and sat in the back of the room while the orchestra rehearsed.

When it was our turn we moved toward the choir loft. I forgot about the podium in the center aisle. It was temporarily placed there for the conductor. I caught my toe on it and tumbled into the orchestra, scattering stands, music, instruments and assorted water bottles.

I'm nearing 90 and my skin is fragile. as are several other parts of my body. The skin tore in three places, requiring several bandages to stop the bleeding. It was enough to get me home, but my neighbor, an emergency-room physician, put on the really big bandage.

Now I know why my family doctor has to ask those questions like whether we have rugs in the house or furniture we have to walk around.

We have furniture in the house, and naturally, we walk around it. Otherwise, I would have a matching bandage on the other arm.

What he should ask is, "Do you have a conductor's podium in your house that you have to walk around?"

I would have to say that I don't but if I did, I probably would stumble over it and fall into the orchestra. We don't really have an orchestra. Our house is too small for anything but a combo. The embarrassment was worse than the pain, but it taught me that if there is an orchestra in the room, watch where you step.

FOLKS LURK BEHIND THE BARN AND LAUGH AT MY SHORTS

IF YOU HAVEN'T NOTICED, it's summer, and that means the pollen count is soaring and we are sneezing more. Worse, our thoughts turn to the wearing of shorts.

Shorts are fine for lithe, young girls with long legs and knobbyless knees. It's another pot of porridge for us older folks. Some of us have short legs and ample bodies. For us, shorts can be a disaster.

Top them off with sandals and white socks and we are left longing for 20 below zero.

Most of the shorts I buy are made for long people who have a lot of space between their belt and their ankles. Most shorts extend about a fourth of the way to their knees. The same clothing extends all the way to the knees of short people. So we are forced to wear semi-shorts.

The distance between the bottom of the shorts and the top of the white socks is about nine inches (I measured). That leaves a pretty small amount of skin for the summer breezes to fall upon.

All of this makes me a bit self-conscious. I'm okay in the house where only my wife sees me. But now and then I have to venture outside, and though we live out in the country on 20 acres, I can sense people lurking behind the barn giggling at my bare legs.

It gets worse when I go somewhere like the hardware store. I tip-toe out the back door, glancing to the right and left. I can almost hear the laughter. Even a smart aleck squirrel is staring at me.

So I sneak back into the house and put on a pair of pants.

So what can be done? It's probably a bit extreme, but we could make wearing shorts a felony, or at least a misdemeanor.

For example, in 1959, the city council of Plattsburgh, N.Y., voted to ban the wearing of shorts by anyone over 16 on city streets. Violators were liable to receive a $25 fine or 25 days in jail.

Other towns have tried similar bans and coolness of legs won out every time. But times are changing. Some companies now allow employees to wear shorts and they're common in some sports.

Tennis players and soccer teams wear shorts but baseball players stick to long pants. Maybe it has something to do with sliding into second base.

Some young people wear jeans with no knees in them.

They're essentially wearing shorts and long pants at the same time.

I've concluded that I'm just not a shorts kind of guy—unless they're on someone else.

I'll wear them around the house because we have plenty of rooms to hide in if someone rings the doorbell. And, if that squirrel smiles the next time I see him, I'll hide all the walnuts that fall off our trees and hope someone buys him a pair of sandals and some little white socks.

IF YOU'RE A SLIDING DANCER DON'T WEAR RUBBER SOLES

WHEN WE WERE in south Texas to visit relatives some time ago we went to a dance. Texans will dance to country music any time and any place—even in a barnyard.

Mostly, they dance the Texas two-step—in cowboy boots. Being a Yankee, or as they say in south Texas, damn Yankee, I had nothing but athletic shoes.

You can stomp pretty well in Reeboks but you can't slide, and I'm a slider. Texans would as soon be caught in athletic shoes as in a pickup truck without a hunting rifle.

So I had to go into Edinburg and buy a pair of shoes. I didn't want to pay a lot so I went to one of those buy-one-and-get-one-free stores. I found loafers for $35. They seemed to fit, so I bought them.

I hadn't noticed the non-slide rubber soles, and after the second or third dance they seemed to grow in size. I also hadn't noticed that they were made in China. Apparently, the Chinese aren't concerned with accurate sizes; they figure Americans are going to wear them anyway.

The generous sizing was good because the arch in one foot doesn't arch and I wear inserts to avoid pain in my heel. The Chinese shoes are big enough for my foot, the insert, and maybe a spare shoe.

I have worn them any time I think I'm going to do a lot of walking or standing. So the part that looks like leather (everything except the sole) is cracking and shows cloth beneath the leather-like surface. You'd think for $35, you'd get something that looks more like leather when it wears out.

When Henry's was a downtown store in Wichita, I bought shoes during the "crazy" sales. I bought really good shoes on sale for $50 and I'm still wearing them (naturally, I take them off when I go to bed).

Shoes have been around for thousands of years. In Mesopotamia, (c. 1600-1200 BC) a type of soft shoes were worn by mountain people who lived near Iran. When these Mesopotamians did a rain dance, it became the first soft-shoe routine.

Sandals were the most common footwear worn by the ancients and they're still worn today, though they are actually different sandals.

I have a pair of sandals nearly as old as those Mesopotamian ones. I wear them in the summer, and they're comfortable. Not being fashion savvy, I wear white socks with them, knowing that I am being stared at wherever I go.

I've seen people wearing flip-flops with socks. The socks are like a glove with a place for the big toe. A strap separates the big toe from the one next to it.

It's like having a two-by-four between your toes.

But your feet are really cool.

IF I CAN'T FIND THE SAW
I CAN'T CUT OFF A FINGER

SINCE I WAS ABOUT 12 years old (quite a while ago) I have been trying to get organized. You know—hang my coat on the same hanger every time so that I will always know where it is when winter comes.

I always find it eventually, but it's often in the summer when I don't really need it. Sometimes I'm tempted to wear it anyway even if I sweat a little because I don't want to waste finding a garment.

I have bought books on how to manage time and how to make lists with priorities. Unfortunately, I usually misplace the books. I keep a notebook with one item on the first page. It says, "get organized."

Over the years I have pretty much decided to live with my disarray. Unfortunately, I haven't convinced my wife to live with it. She keeps nagging me about my messy office—just because she can't find her way to my desk (I'm sure it's still in there).

My woodworking shop is kind of messy, too, but I figure that's good because I can't get through the debris to my saw. Obviously that's a safety feature. If I can't get to my saw, I can't cut off a finger—or a toe should I lose my balance.

One day I decided I'd had enough and set out to organize the shop. It would be a thing of beauty with everything in its place. I cut out a piece of wood and drilled holes in it to hold all of my screwdrivers. I couldn't find any screwdrivers. Next, I picked up all the wood scraps strewn about the floor. I put them back because you never know when you're going to need a small scrap of wood for something.

Next, I looked at all that sawdust on the floor and pretty much everywhere else. I turned on my shop vacuum but nothing happened because it wasn't plugged in. That was because all of the outlets had something plugged into them. Some of the outlets are behind heavy machinery which doesn't matter because I can't get to them anyway.

I decided that if I wore a dust mask, I could just leave the dust—that is if I had a dust mask.

I did some research on organization. One piece of advice I turned up was that the process of organizing "really comes down to having a system for automating decisions about where everything goes".

Well, duh! I've been doing that all along. When I have an object I don't have a place for, I throw it in a pile in the corner. When that corner is full there still are three more. That's not so difficult.

Another tip I came across says to do away with duplication. "Why have two nonstick spatulas when one is enough?"

The answer to that is you need two because one of them is in the dishwasher, and a person who needs help with clutter does not turn on a dishwasher until nothing more can be crammed into it.

I almost forgot. You can't write a learned treatise without defining something. So here it is: the dictionary says that clutter is "to make disorderly or hard to use by filling or covering with objects."

By that definition, buying a plastic box at the department store to reduce clutter and filling it with objects that are cluttering your office or bedroom or kitchen actually is cluttering. And, if you cover the box with something to hide it, you are cluttering again.

So to avoid a mess, leave the stuff where it is. This is the way I have been dealing with clutter all my life. It makes sense to me.

CAROUSING AND PARTIES
HAVE LOST SOME APPEAL

WE WERE ATTENDING a party not long ago. My wife and I do this occasionally although we tend to choose parties that are less boisterous than might have been evident a few years ago.

The soirees we attend are nearly unbearably free of clatter and commotion. The only noise is the occasional peanut some clumsy guest lets fall to the floor. There is always a designated driver—for guests who haven't yet scheduled their cataract operations.

These parties usually involve dinner and a glass of wine before and during dinner. These shindigs can last until 9 or 9:30 p.m., and the adventurous ones will often drink a cup of coffee.

We don't carouse any more—if we ever did. The word comes from the German and dates to the 1500s when people probably did a lot more carousing than we do today. Originally it meant "time to leave the bar or a last drink before closing time."

Our idea of a big night these days is to sit down with a bowl of popcorn and a Netflix (no R rated ones, of course). If we're feeling particularly decadent, we add extra butter.

It's ironic that as retirees, Saturday night hasn't the significance it once had. We don't have to get up early to drive to work—or anywhere. So we could as easily party on Wednesday night, that is if we wanted to party at all.

Our ideas of what is entertaining change. When I was a high school student I looked forward to Independence Day. It meant seeing my friends and celebrating at a sunrise dance or something of the sort.

I recall one Fourth of July when I was in a dance band that we played in one town from 9 p.m. to midnight then drove 75 miles to play for dancers even crazier than we were from 2 a.m. to sunrise. The disappointment was that there weren't any parties to go to at sunrise.

Now I'm more interested in the patriotic significance of the holiday and I dread the noise that begins a week before and extends a week or so after the Fourth.

New Year's Eve was another good holiday in my younger days. In the early 1940s I often played the trumpet for dances.

I worked at a dry goods Store after school and on Saturdays.

The routine in those pre-computer days was to count everything in the store on New Year's Eve—a decided damper on holiday festivities.

It was the last day of 1943 as near as I can recall and the manager of the local power company office, a dance-band drummer, called me over to his office about three doors north of the dry goods store. He had a job to play for a New Year's dance at a country club 30 miles away. He had rounded up a piano, bass fiddle and electric guitar and he needed a "horn." He asked me to play for the dance.

I went to my boss and asked if I could skip the inventory. "You can play for the dance or do inventory and keep your job," he said.

At that time music was more important to me than a job, so I chose to play my trumpet. I probably did the wrong thing but I'm glad I did it.

That night we set up our little combo on the dance floor and an exuberant dancer bumped into my horn and split my lip. I played the last hour and a half out of the side of my mouth.

As I write this there are holidays ahead, and the celebration of them is a bit different. Our only granddaughter is an occupational therapist in Dallas and will drive to our house for Christmas. And, our three "children," now all in their 50s and 60s, will be here with their families and they'll be scratching their heads trying to come up with an appropriate gift for a Dad in his 80s.

I can tell them that there is no appropriate gift for such a person. I have everything I am nimble enough to use. I don't play golf and even if I did, I would quit. I like tools but I can't cut into a piece of wood without creating a coughing spell. Besides, anything I could make would not be very useful.

In other words, the party season no longer is for partying at our place. Just having our far-flung family together for even a short time is party enough—and I plan to enjoy it.

KETCHUP ON MAC AND CHEESE SHOULD BE ILLEGAL

OUR SON AND DAUGHTER-IN-LAW came over for dinner recently and we served macaroni and cheese. There is nothing particularly strange about that, but what they put on it was something else.

They slathered on (gasp) ketchup.

Now, I'm not averse to a little ketchup on my French fries, but mac and cheese? Next they'll be dousing their ice cream with it.

I made a comment about this and they countered with, "If you can put peanut butter on pancakes, why can't we put ketchup on mac and cheese?"

I didn't say it, but the logical answer is peanut butter on pancakes tastes good. Ketchup on mac and cheese is an abomination. The yellow cheese and red ketchup make a dull orange that if not inedible, it looks like it.

It got me to thinking about the other weird things people put on their food and the strange ways some of them want it prepared. My brother-in-law has explicit instructions on how he wants his sandwiches made. You start with bread slathered with mayo, lettuce next to the bread, then the tomatoes on the lettuce. The meat rests on the tomatoes, then the second piece of bread completes it. He won't eat it if it's made any other way.

Some people put ketchup on bananas and others put jelly on cheeseburgers. Others dip their fries in chocolate ice cream. Believe it or not, there are misdirected folks who eat peanut butter and tomato sandwiches, and others consume peanut butter and dill pickle sandwiches and I've heard of a kid who eats peanut butter and bologna on toast.

One person drinks pickle juice and another dips potato chips in melted ice cream. Fresh popcorn with milk eaten like cereal turns some people on, while others make a sandwich of bacon and grape jelly on toast.

Elvis made fried banana and peanut butter sandwiches. He made them with white bread, two tablespoons of butter and two tablespoons of peanut butter. It was fried like a toasted cheese sandwich.

Presley once flew 800 miles to eat a sandwich made of a whole loaf of Italian bread, peanut butter, jelly and a pound of bacon.

Other weird food combinations include Cheetos and milk, peanut butter and pickle sandwich, salami and grapes, salt and pepper on apples, fries dipped in honey and peanut butter and onion sandwich.

The strangeness continues with Oreos dipped in orange juice, vanilla ice cream with soy sauce, grape jelly and scrambled eggs, popcorn and marshmallows, and strawberries with sour cream and brown sugar.

Pregnant women take the cake (with ketchup on it, of course) when it comes to weird food combinations. One woman said she ate chocolate ice cream with banana peppers.

If they weren't so tasty, you might consider s'mores funny food. It's a marshmallow blackened over an open fire on a graham cracker and piece of chocolate bar.

When I was a kid my grandmother gave me butter and sugar on bread and a glass of buttermilk to go with it.

What's strange about that?

IF YOU'RE A DREAMER
TRY TO DREAM GOOD STUFF

NO COLUMNIST WORTH his salt should go through life without writing about dreams. In ancient days, a columnist worth his salt would be wealthy. These days we think nothing of sprinkling salt on French fries or tossing it over our shoulder for good luck. There was a day when it was highly prized because it was scarce. Without it, food would spoil and explorers would not have found any new lands, say, in New Zealand.

For a number of years after college I had a recurring dream. It varied but the theme was always the same. I was signed up for a class but didn't know what time it met nor where it was held.

Each night I freaked out because I didn't know where my class was. I finally decided it probably was a class I would flunk anyway.

Let's look into some other common dreams. Some people dream about birds. The psychologists say (they know a lot about birds) if you dream about birds, you have aspirations and wish to rise above your troubles.

The psychologists don't say what these troubles are, but they could be that you have parked your car under a tree and an uncouth bird or birds have made a mess on it. You probably are going to dream of swinging a bat at them—but not while they're still sitting on your car.

Another common dream is that you are walking around in a public place—say a shopping mall—and you are naked.

Obviously, this is not a good idea. If you are sleepy, you probably will want to shower with your clothes on and look carefully at yourself in the mirror before you go to the mall.

Another popular dream is that you are flying—usually without an airplane. The nice thing is that the person in front of you does not lower his seat and squeeze you into a tiny ball. That's because that person is actually a duck flying south.

Some people dream about losing their teeth. The dream interpreters don't say whether these are real teeth or false teeth.

I'm thinking false teeth would be a lot easier to lose than your real teeth, but I'm not a psychologist.

To dream can mean something you want to happen but isn't likely. For example: "I dream that this guy will write a column that makes sense."

You have just dreamed the impossible dream.

But let's stop being facetious (a funny word). A Boston sleep scientist says that a dream may be weaving new material into the memory system in a way that helps us cope with stressful events.

So let's say you got a parking ticket, certainly a stressful event, and you go to sleep and dream that you are naked in the shopping mall. You awaken and find that you are fully clothed and are not in the shopping mall. That reduces a lot of stress right away.

ABOUT THE AUTHOR

Ted Blankenship is a retired journalist who has been a reporter, photographer, Sunday editor, city editor, managing editor and editorial writer on Kansas newspapers. He has also been an adjunct professor at Wichita State University and Friends University. He writes a monthly column for The Active Age, a newspaper for Kansans 50 and older.

57343863R00068

Made in the USA
Middletown, DE
17 December 2017